THIS COULD BE YOUR DAY

THIS
COULD
BE
YOUR
DAY

A Christopher "THREE-MINUTES-A-DAY" Book

THE CHRISTOPHERS
12 EAST 48TH STREET
NEW YORK, N.Y. 10017

ABOUT THE CHRISTOPHERS

We are a mass-media organization which uses the printed word, television and radio to spread two basic ideas:

There's nobody like you.
You can make a difference.

Based on the Judeo-Christian concept of service to God and all humanity, the Christopher message is addressed to people of all faiths and of no particular faith.

We believe . . .

■ That you are a unique person.

■ That your community, nation and world need what you have to give.

■ That fault-finding has its place, but that constructive action is the best and most lasting response to the shortcomings of society.

■ That each of us is called by God to become personally and actively involved in seeking solutions to the problems that confront us all.

■ That each of us is entrusted with a job to do—one that has been given to no one else.

■ That whoever and wherever we are, each of us has an opportunity to help shape the world we live in.

■ That the basic approach is summed up in the words: "Be not overcome by evil, but overcome evil with good." (Romans 12:21)

The Christophers is a non-profit organization. We have no branches, no meetings, no dues. To meet our expenses, we depend on voluntary donations from people who believe that the individual can make a difference. We get no funding from church or government sources. All gifts are welcome—and deductible from taxable income.

The Christopher motto is an ancient Chinese proverb: "Better to light one candle than to curse the darkness."

To find out more about The Christophers—or to receive our News Notes free of charge seven times a year, write to:

The Christophers
Father Ronald Saucci, M.M., Acting Director
12 East 48th Street
New York, NY 10017
212-759-4050

LOOK AT YOUR LIFE

**"The man who has begun
to live more seriously within
begins to live more simply without."
—Ernest Hemingway**

In the last century, a tourist from America paid a visit to a renowned Polish rabbi, Hofetz Chaim.

He was astonished to see that the rabbi's home was only a simple room filled with books, plus a table and a bench.

"Rabbi," asked the tourist, "where is your furniture?"

"Where is yours?" replied Hofetz Chaim.

"Mine?" asked the puzzled American. "But I'm only a visitor here. I'm only passing through."

"So am I," said the rabbi.

● ● ●

Experienced travelers learn how much baggage is just enough. They take what they need and leave behind the non-essentials that would only be a burden. To move freely, they travel light.

Visitor, traveler, pilgrim—whatever word we use—each one of us is "passing through."

How we go through life depends a lot on what each of us decides is essential in the things we own, the attachments we form, the ideas that shape our lives.

A CHANGE IN DIRECTION?

More and more people say they'd like to make changes in the way they live.

Following a recent poll, Louis Harris commented that we may be coming to the point "where the accumulation of physical possessions and steadily increasing consumption would no longer be as central to people's concerns . . . This would mark a striking turnabout in the country's thinking."

But any major change in the way we live is going to require decisions by millions of individuals, in their personal and public lives, in answer to the question: "How do I want to travel?"

REDUCING THE LOAD

On a personal level, questions like these may be helpful to anyone who is serious about finding out what to hold onto and what to let go:

■ What possessions do I have that cause more trouble and worry than they're worth?

■ Do I weigh myself down by longing for more than I need or can afford?

■ Do I waste valuable time and energy on things that don't really matter?

■ Does the desire for "bigger, better, more" crowd

out the values of intimacy, communication and the giving of affection?

- ■ Do I feel good about my work, the persons in my life, myself?
- ■ If I had only three months to live, what would I let go of and what would I hold onto?

> "If I am
> what I have
> —and if what I have
> is lost
> who then am I?"
> —Erich Fromm

TRAVELING LIGHT

Simply—Maggie and David Cavagnaro left the world of competition and overconsumption to become resident biologists at a California wildlife sanctuary. Relying more on their own efforts than outside resources, they find themselves more open to nature's rhythms. "We live simply without," said Maggie, "so that we might be less encumbered on our larger journey within."

Economically—A priest in upstate New York began using a bicycle on his parish rounds. Father Anthony Keller finds it faster in traffic, cheaper than a car—and good exercise. He says he's meeting more people and getting closer to their needs.

Independently—A Georgia couple decided to cut consumption, grow their own vegetables, bake bread and make more things themselves. Mr. and Mrs. Peter Mann buy only necessary clothing and household goods. "I feel so much freer," says Arlene Mann.

Moderately—An English couple in their fifties have moved from London to a country cottage and reduced consumption. They eat less, throw away less and make do with less. Says Patrick Rivers, "We no longer feel trapped in the consumer society."

Thoughtfully—After making a lot of money as a young man, Morgan Maxfield of Missouri decided there was more to life than a big income. He sold most of his business interests and involved himself in community projects. "I've watched people turn money into a god, and I don't want to do that," he says. "There are much better things to do."

Politically—In 1974, some concerned people in New York formed Bread for the World, an organization that prods members of Congress to adopt policies favorable to feeding the hungry at home and overseas. Membership has grown to over 15,000. "Global citizenship," says director Arthur Simon, a Lutheran pastor, "is not new to Christianity."

> "What gain then is it
> for a man to
> win the whole world
> and ruin his life?"
> —Jesus

EXCESS BAGGAGE—A GLOBAL VIEW

In a recent speech, Barbara Ward, the British economist and environmentalist, offered a global perspective on the need to live simply.

Ms. Ward told an audience in Vancouver, B.C., that the real issues facing the world were not matters of diplomacy but "daily bread, shelter, water, work . . . the ability to live on this planet in such a way that we don't destroy it."

"We live in the world of privilege," she said, "the world of good fortune, the world of prosperity, and this world we are going to have to share with about three to four billion more people of whom at least two-thirds are going to have annual incomes of less than $250 per year."

The British economist cited the Jewish prophets, ". . . all of whom were proponents of a moral sense of obligation to the poor and a judgment on the unmindful and uncaring rich . . ."

Ms. Ward reminded her hearers:

■ People in the wealthy nations throw away 15 percent of all the food they buy.

■ Modern glass-enclosed skyscrapers waste energy by using only about one-quarter of the heat generated. "The twin 100-story towers of New York's World Trade Center," she said, "consume as much energy in a day as the entire city of Pittsburgh."

■ $300 billion are spent on armaments each year. "One B-1 bomber," she pointed out, "uses up as much gasoline in one year as the entire bus fleet of the United States."

The British author appealed for personal action, "the law of conscience," and political action, "the law of the community."

"We will survive as a human community only if we can see the needs of others, and only if we will keep power—including our own powerful desires—under some restraint and under some rule of law. The law of conscience and the law of the community."

"I have learned to manage
on whatever I have.
I know how to be poor
and how to be rich . . .
There is nothing I cannot master
with the help
of the One who gives me strength."
—St. Paul

GETTING THERE . . .

If we know where we're going, we can better prepare for the journey.

These "travel" tips may be helpful:

Keep your sense of direction—Take time out occasionally to consult your inner compass—your own best self.

Observe the speed limits—Set a pace that won't burn you out before you reach your destination.

Watch the road signs—Each day there are indications of danger, directions on how to proceed, signs of progress. Look for them. Respond to them.

Stop, look and listen—Pay attention to the task you are doing and the person you are with.

Be concerned for the other travelers—Give support and encouragement to others.

Refuel—Make it a regular practice to read the Bible and other spiritual books. Pray.

SCRAPING OFF THE BARNACLES

Tiny crustaceans no bigger than walnuts can slow down a ship weighing thousands of tons. Within six months after it goes into the water, a vessel may acquire two or three inches of these barnacles. The layer can weigh 100 tons and reduce a ship's speed by more than 10 percent.

The only way to get rid of the annoying creatures is to haul the vessel out of the water and scrape them off. Sometimes it takes a jackhammer.

People can also acquire "barnacles." We get so weighed down that our progress as human beings is impeded—and other people suffer too.

Human life has often been compared to a journey, whether by land or sea. It can be rocky, stormy, uncertain. But, at every stage, we have the divine assurance that we are not alone. He who is with us is the One who waits to greet us at journey's end.

W̶E HAVE COME ACROSS the following words by W. Heartsill Wilson, entitled "A Prayer For Today."

"This is the beginning of a new day.

"God has given me this day to use as I will.

"I can waste it—or use it for good, but what I do today is important, because I am exchanging a day of my life for it!

"When tomorrow comes, this day will be gone forever, leaving in its place something that I have traded for it.

"I want it to be gain, and not loss; good, and not evil; success, and not failure; in order that I shall not regret the price that I have paid for it."

This day is all we have. Is there someone to whom an act of kindness—not tomorrow but today—could make a world of difference?

Today, whether we spend it well or throw it away, will be gone tomorrow. What is there to do that is worth our effort?

> "The day is at hand."   [ROMANS 13:12]

    Lord, may we seek You in the present moment.

S ERGIO LATORRE AND LARRY BRENNER are "Lemon Detectors." The two New York men are travelling auto-diagnosticians, who help tell potential used-car buyers if an auto is any good.

Charging from $20 to $30, the men test engine, transmission and even whole-car performance. Their experience, says Mr. Brenner, shows there are two basic kinds of used-car dealers.

"The honest dealer won't bother with a dent or two in a fender. He'll sell it because it's a good buy. But there's another type of hustler who specializes in buying wrecked or repossessed cars for little money." This type he says, turns mileage back, doctors up the outside and sells the car with its engine on its last cough. That's the fellow, say the two men, that their service is designed to detect.

If we had an honest world, we wouldn't need lemon detectors—or police, prisons and truant officers. As it is, we can be grateful for those who try to keep human dealings "on the level." And we can do so ourselves.

> "He who speaks the truth gives honest evidence."   [PROVERBS 12:17]

℣ Help me make the world a better place, Lord, beginning with me.

W HEN EL PASO, ILLINOIS, lost its central telephone system, its 2,291 residents knew they'd lost a whole way of life.

In a pushbutton age, the tiny hamlet was one of the last Illinois towns to end its three-number system with the friendly voice at the other end.

Before the changeover to the dial system, folks knew the voices at Central as Amy, Ferne, Eleanor, Gladys or Clio. On election night, Amy could tell you who was leading for the school board. If the person you called for was out to lunch, Ferne could ring the Gala Restaurant.

"Sure, I'll miss the personal touch," says a local insurance broker, "but you can't stand in the way of progress." Progress is at best a mixed blessing. Each of us can find ways to keep the "personal touch" no matter what the future brings. We can listen, encourage, cheer, grieve with others. No machine can do that, and no human being can do without it.

"Comfort one another."
[1 THESSALONIANS 4:18]

   Make us more conscious, Lord, that growth as caring persons is a vital goal in our lives.

SMOKING ONE CIGARETTE on a Chicago Transit Authority train netted an arrest and one year's court supervision for one rider.

It wasn't that the CTA's no-smoking rule was that strict, however. Police said that 43-year-old William Riley, a restaurant worker, boarded the train puffing a cigarette. When Virginia Cronk, a police officer travelling incognito on decoy duty, asked Riley to put it out, he blew smoke in her face.

Officer Cronk arrested Riley, and when searched, he was found to be carrying a $600 carton of stolen steaks.

Arrogance has no place in the dealings between civilized human beings. It's doubly out of order when we're in the wrong to begin with. Yet, isn't it usually to cover doubts or downright error that we resort to bluster and bravado?

How peculiar our motivations can be. Think about it.

"Show perfect courtesy toward all men."
[TITUS 3:2]

≥§ Father, may we treat each other with respect at all times.

A YOUNG WOMAN DYING of leukemia sent this plea to columnist Ann Landers:

1. Treat me the same as a well person. Don't ask me, "How are you doing?"

2. Include me in your activities. I need friends just as you do.

3. Forget I have a disease. I'll do better if I don't know it's on your mind.

4. Ask me out. You can even marry me. I might live another 20 years.

5. Hire me. If I'm productive, I will live longer.

6. Get a check-up this week. Many forms of cancer can be cured if caught early.

7. Treat me as you would like to be treated under the same circumstances.

8. Love me! Enjoy me! I have a lot to give.

Our fears are painful and may lead us to inflict hurt on others. Love and understanding can replace fear.

"There is no fear in love, but perfect love casts out fear." [1 JOHN 4:18]

ᴇ§ Help me, Holy Spirit, to pay less attention to people's differences than to what we have in common.

AFTER FORTY MILLION YEARS in the sea, the world's largest creature, the whale, is heading for extinction.

The blue whale tops them all—100 feet long and over 100 tons in weight. The huge mammal swims freely in the sea, feeding only on tiny crustaceans. It has one natural enemy—any shark that goes after its young.

Adults spend a year raising an "infant." The monogamous creature risks death to comfort a fatally wounded mate.

His good will extends even to humans. A blue whale takes utmost care not to upset a small boat. But humans may hunt the ocean giants into extinction.

Man is the only creature capable of destroying the earth and everything that lives. But humanity—people like you and me—can also transform this world into something far better.

Each of us has some part to play. What's your choice?

> "For from the greatness and beauty of created things comes a corresponding perception of their Creator."   [WISDOM 13:5]

⋞ Bring us to a deeper appreciation of all Your creatures, Father, great and small.

HEN GABRIELLE, 3, returned to the Angel Guardian Home in Brooklyn, New York, from a foster home, she was so upset she couldn't eat.

So Sister Mary Paul, who was then director of adoptions at the home, phoned Eva and Lenny Johnson. Without children of their own, the couple had already adopted another little girl.

The Johnsons took in Gabrielle. Then they went on to adopt two boys. "They communicate their love and happiness to everyone they meet," said one of the Sisters about the Johnsons.

"Many couples are reluctant to adopt children," says Mr. Johnson, "because they are afraid of the responsibility. But our experience has been, that if you rely on God, He provides whatever you need."

God does provide. Whether it's giving love to a homeless child, or settling international disputes, reliance on God is an effective remedy for fear of taking on responsibility. Ask for faith—you'll surely get it.

> "If you have faith as a grain of mustard seed . . . nothing will be impossible to you."
> [MATTHEW 17:20]

∝ May we put our trust in You, Father, where it belongs.

WHETHER YOU'RE SPEAKING to the State Legislature or a small group of friends, these pointers by writer Vince Vinci may help:

■ Know your audience. What sort of individuals are they? Age? Affluence? Interests? Then tailor your speech to them, touching their common ground.

■ Think big. Keep your visuals, your gestures, pictorial and dramatic.

■ Tap their memories, experiences, senses. Don't say "house" when "grey, weather-beaten cottage" can put them right at the edge of the picture.

■ Give loving care to the organization of your presentation. Tell them what you are going to say. Say it. Tell them what you have said. Repeat. Connect. Emphasize. Keep it constantly tied together.

People can quickly tell whether we really have regard for our audience, or merely tolerate them. Many skills are needed for effective communication, but love for people is at the root of them all.

"Let your speech always be gracious, seasoned with salt, so that you may know how you ought to answer every one."
[COLOSSIANS 4:6]

❧ Lord, help me to season my speech with love of others.

I T TOOK A GROUP OF 4-year-olds to bridge the generation gap in Mill Valley, California.

For several weeks the children attending the Tamalpais Nursery School watched the elderly people at the Redwoods Retirement Home across the street. Many were in wheelchairs or hobbling about with canes.

When one of the tots suggested, "Let's visit those old ladies across the street," the nursery school teacher decided it would be a good idea.

Now, one day each week, the pupils visit their "neighbors" at Redwoods—an occasion that brings smiles to the faces of both old and young.

Nobody—young, old; black, white; male, female— has a monopoly on good ideas. That's why it's so important to encourage everyone to look for human needs and ways to satisfy them.

That's why we at The Christophers say: "Better to light one candle than to curse the darkness." Any ideas?

"If there is anything worthy of praise, think about these things." [PHILIPPIANS 4:8]

৶ Holy Spirit, may we use our imaginations.

IN RACINE, WISCONSIN, crying in your beer may get you the help you need.

In the city's 157 taverns, bartenders are being trained as "mental health referral agents" in a pilot program sponsored by the Racine County Mental Health Association. Despondent, troubled patrons are gently steered to professional help by barmen who learn in a 15-hour course to spot and tactfully assist depressed or belligerent customers.

The "referral agents" follow three basic rules:

■ Don't moralize.

■ Make sure the patron wants to be helped.

■ Never contact the counselor for the patron. The motivation must come from within.

You don't need to be an expert to help people, except maybe an expert in compassion. But you do need to know how much you can and can't do.

Maybe the best thing we can do is to listen carefully so that people can lower their defenses and find courage to seek assistance on their own.

> "If you will not listen, my soul will weep in secret."   [JEREMIAH 13:17]

✍ Keep us from going through life with tunnel-vision, Lord, failing to see opportunities to help.

DR. MARY LEAKEY, a leading anthropologist and widow of Dr. Louis Leakey, has found human fossils in East Africa 3.75 million years old. That would make homo sapiens a million years older than was previously thought.

To put it another way, if a generation is 20 years, then 750,000 generations of human beings and related species have lived since those fossils were alive. It has been a mere 600 generations since the ancient Egyptians built the Sphinx and the Pyramids 3,000 years ago.

Seen in the perspective of millions of years, today's triumphs and tragedies may seem pretty small. But there are other ways to measure value. One is at the personal level: one human being helping—or failing to help—another.

Our faith and our common sense tell us that we are important, that we can make a difference. To whom will our actions this day make a difference for the better?

> "Like a drop of water from the sea and a grain of sand so are a few years in the day of eternity." [SIRACH 18:10]

⁖ Help us daily, Father, to distill the essence of life, to minimize the unimportant.

W HEN THE TOWN COUNCIL of Surprise, Arizona, need to get something done, they just say, "Let George do it," and he does. George is Mayor George Cumbie.

Mayor Cumbie, 54-year-old, four-term mayor of the little farming community of 4,000, is personally responsible for paving its 50 streets. Mr. Cumbie, a paving contractor, was faced with a town of dusty, unpaved roads when he took over as mayor in 1968. Looking over the town's modest budget and the high cost of road improvements, he decided that the only way to put an end to the dust clouds was to donate the paving himself.

Many forms of "letting George do it" don't have such happy results.

Every level of public service, from the humblest to the highest, needs people who will go the extra mile in the interests of the wider community.

It's only natural to complain about public figures who don't do their jobs. But it makes just as much sense to ask ourselves when was the last time we made a sacrifice for the good of all.

> "I heard the voice of the Lord saying, 'Whom shall I send?' . . . Then I said, 'Here I am! Send me.' " [ISAIAH 6:8,9]

> ◄§ Keep us, Holy Spirit, from taking short cuts that would take away the rights of others.

Pawn tickets, old silver and cash totaling $50,000 were an aged New York woman's gift of gratitude to a student who helped her.

The wealth, given by Mrs. Ethel Field to 19-year-old John Bianchi before and after her death at 81, was her reward to Mr. Bianchi for visiting her daily to heat her dinner and run errands for her.

A college student who earned $40 as a part-time grocery clerk, Mr. Bianchi was astonished by Mrs. Field's bequests to him as her only heir.

"It's like something I guess you dream about that really comes true," he said. "She never complained about anything. Doing things for someone like that is more or less a pleasure. Even if she wasn't wealthy I would have helped her out."

If it always paid to be thoughtful, we'd have reason to question our motives. As it is, our kindness sometimes goes unnoticed, except by Him to whom we must all render an account. Maybe it's better that way.

> "I am He who searches mind and heart, and I will give to each of you as your works deserve." [REVELATIONS 2:23]

ぺる Give us an outlook of helpfulness, Lord, which doesn't seek a reward.

A PEN AND PAPER are all it takes to give hope and direction to forgotten men and women through the Fortune Society's Pen-Pal program.

Now in its third year, the program has matched over 4,000 prisoners with civilian pen-pals. Demand is so great that the waiting time is from three to five months for each prisoner, because of the shortage of civilian pen-pals.

The Fortune Society matches inmates and civilians, and sends prison writing regulations. If you're interested, contact The Fortune Society, 29 E. 22nd St., NYC 10010. It can be the first step.

Research seems to prove that only one thing really helps ex-prisoners "go straight": the personal concern of another individual.

You can make a start towards safer streets and a healthier society by showing one former convict that you care. It can begin with a letter. With God's help, it can end with a new friendship.

> "There is nothing so precious as a faithful friend, and no scales can measure his excellence." [SIRACH 6:15]

> Strengthen us, Father, to extend the hand of friendship to someone who needs what we can give.

WLBT-TV OF JACKSON, Mississippi, is the only television station in the United States to have had its license revoked because of a civil rights suit.

In 1964, Jackson civil rights leaders and the United Church of Christ challenged a renewal application, charging discriminatory practices—a low level of minority hiring and absence of news affecting the poor and blacks. On appeal, the license was revoked.

A Jackson-based group, Communications Improvement, Inc., received an interim license and pledged 40 percent black employment. Today WLBT-TV has a biracial board of directors. Says General Manager Bill Dilday:

"The important thing is that this station is on top though we've been hiring young blacks off the street with no experience and training them on the job."

People usually say it can't be done—until somebody does it. How many times do our fears hold back our abilities?

> "Be a vessel for noble use, consecrated and useful . . . ready for any good work."
> [2 TIMOTHY 2:21]

✝ Make us more conscious of what we can do, Lord, in the midst of obstacles.

An INNOVATIVE TEACHER in a New Jersey high school has taken handicapped students "off the shelf." They no longer sit in study hall during gym class or on the sidelines during sports activities.

William Librera has started a class just for them. Students with limitations ranging from brain damage to bone ailments do exercise and use a weight-lifting machine adjustable to their strengths. Some go on to tennis, archery, softball or badminton.

Mr. Librera was moved by concern about the psychological damage to the youngster who feels "out of it." Besides sheer enjoyment, he feels students will build confidence that comes from competence.

"I'm convinced that every child in the public schools," says Mr. Librera, "is entitled to a physical education program for his specific need."

Each of us occasionally senses an injustice, pain or need. If we don't act, the moment passes. Think about it.

"Go, do all that is in your heart; for the Lord is with you." [2 SAMUEL 7:3]

  Help me, Father, to overcome the inertia that prevents me from being really helpful.

Dionesia Perez has been singing and laughing for 116 years. That, she says, is the secret of living.

Mrs. Perez, born New Year's Day, 1860, was given a special birthday party by five generations of her family and 35 public officials at the Concourse Nursing Home in the Bronx. To the nearly 100 well-wishers, the little Puerto Rican woman gave this advice:

"Sing, sing and be happy. Sing and say a few prayers to the Virgin and you'll see how things get better. I was raised in the midst of music."

"I think she's beautiful," commented a nurse. "She never cries, never complains. Everything about her is laughter."

Mrs. Perez is blind and hard of hearing but still enjoys singing and cheering up other residents.

Cheering up others is a way to keep happy yourself. Give it a try and you will add music to life.

> "The fear of the Lord delights the heart, and gives gladness and joy and long life."
> [SIRACH 1:12]

Stir us, Father, to get beyond preoccupation with self.

A SIMPLE MIXTURE that includes glucose (a sugar) and salt may help prevent the death of thousands of cholera sufferers and reduce the effect of severe diarrhea, according to Dr. Eugene Gangerosa of the U.S. Public Health Service.

The treatment has already been used with an unheard-of recovery rate of 50 to 60 percent for cholera victims in Bangladesh.

Massive dehydration accompanies cholera infection. Efforts to restore bodily fluids by ordinary methods are usually unsuccessful. The new mixture is much more readily absorbed by the sick and this helps them fight the disease.

The discovery can't be patented. Since it's not profitable, no U.S. drug company has undertaken to produce it. But it is being produced in India.

If you believe that science should be at the service of human needs, you can raise your voice for the widespread production of a treatment that can save millions of lives. If you won't, who will?

> "Maintain the rights of the afflicted and the destitute." [PSALM 82:3]

෯ Rouse us from apathy, Holy Spirit, and lead us to speak and act in behalf of the defenseless.

A NEW YORK CAB DRIVER takes pictures of his passengers—with their permission. And he asks them to photograph him.

Richard Evans, 24, is a student at the School of Visual Arts. Photography, for him, is more than a hobby. But his unusual practice of combining the click of the meter with that of the camera is a sideline with mixed results.

"It's interesting," says Mr. Evans, "to see how they react to me." Responses range from grudging to gracious. About five percent of his fares hesitate. A few refuse. He learns how people perceive him as a human being by the way they photograph him.

Methods vary: profile, full-face, close-up, distance shots. "A few have gotten out," he says, "and shot me in the cab from the outside."

With or without a camera, the gift of seeing ourselves as others do is rare. It is worth going after because such an "outside view" can help to make us the kind of persons we were created to be.

"Let a man examine himself."
[1 CORINTHIANS 11:28]

≈§ Sharpen our self-awareness, Jesus, so we can get some perspective on ourselves.

THE ENVIRONMENT'S BRAVEST "minority group" is city trees, according to Robert Daismont, tree-planting coordinator for New York City.

It takes determination, he believes, for a tree to survive the onslaughts of traffic, dogs, rock salt, air pollution and concrete. A New York City tree's life expectancy is 10 to 20 years, assuming first-year survival and optimal care, says Mr. Daismont. He noted that along upper Riverside Drive "hardly a tree had not been hit by a car."

Mr. Daismont sees a great need for "urban forestry" experts to refresh and beautify cities.

"Now we are starting to practice 'people forestry' instead of 'tree forestry,' to educate urban people about the uses of vegetation in the city," Mr. Daismont says. "Keeping the complexity and diversity of cities working well is also the key to the management of open land."

Caring for a tree is a small part of caring for a neighborhood. Once we recognize that we can improve our environment by a change in our own attitudes, some beautiful things can happen to it—and to us.

> "Be glad and rejoice forever in that which I create." [ISAIAH 65:18]

Remind us to stop and reflect, Holy Spirit, before we begin to take action.

Since the fifteenth century, the villagers of Gheel, Belgium, have helped thousands of mentally ill patients find health and peace of mind.

In a tradition handed down for generations, many families in Gheel are certified to care for mentally ill patients in their homes. Many patients are encouraged to work, and there are no medical or physical restraints or psychiatric treatments, such as psychotherapy. Patients are treated kindly and humanely, as family members.

In Gheel's 500-year history as a haven for the mentally ill, there has been only one act of violence, and that was a politically motivated murder. The village's recovery rate compares favorably with institutions which are far more expensive.

Tenderness and caring promote healing both of soul and body. If more of us could show a personal concern for those in mental distress, we might alleviate the acute sense of loneliness that goes along with such affliction. It is by giving that we receive.

"I am lonely and afflicted. Relieve the troubles of my heart." [PSALM 25:16]

᪥ Instill in our hearts, Holy Spirit, a tender regard for all persons in difficulty.

BEING "JUST A HOUSEWIFE" in 1776 was a back-breaking job, according to an ad in the *Pennsylvania Packet* that year. It asked for a woman qualified in:

"Raising small stock, dairying, marketing, combing, carding, spinning, knitting, sewing and preserving."

To feed a family 200 years ago was an enormous task. A wife was expected to milk, churn, butcher, salt and smoke meats, render fats, candy fruits, pickle and dry vegetables.

A clean family required soap. To make it involved boiling 24 pounds of grease and six bushels of wood ash for each barrel of lye soap.

Most women added several hours each day tutoring the children, and three or four hours on Sunday at the local meeting house or church.

Each era has its own pressures. It probably wouldn't be accurate to say that men and women today have it easier than in the past—only different. If we recognize that every life has its trials, maybe we can cope better with our own problems.

> "When you meet various trials . . . know that the testing of your faith produces steadfastness."   [JAMES 1:2]

≥§ Give us a healthy respect for the past, Jesus, and a hopeful vision of the future.

A NILES, CALIFORNIA, service station has started selling gasoline by the liter. Patrons get bumper stickers reading, "Go Metric."

Jack Holland, president of a company with many stations in the state, has launched the pilot project in cooperation with the local county government. The metric system, long used in many countries, is deemed simpler and more accurate than other systems. "The question is no longer whether we convert," says Mr. Holland, "but when and how."

Customers driving into the Niles station for five gallons of gas ask for 19 liters, the closest equivalent. "It looks a little complicated at first," says the company president, "put actually it's easier once you get the hang of it."

One we have decided a change is for the better— or inevitable—we usually have the ability to adjust. But the mature person—given the option—also asks, "Is this change really better? Is this a direction worth taking?"

"A man of understanding sets his face toward wisdom." [PROVERBS 17:24]

ᴈ⸱ Holy Spirit, give me the wisdom to judge the value of new directions.

To BENEFIT OTHERS, a bishop told the story of his alcoholism and recovery to the *Omaha World-Herald*.

It was tough for Bishop Robert P. Varley, 53, head of Nebraska's 65 Episcopal parishes and missions. But he said he had learned to value toughness.

Friends told him he was an alcoholic, and he went to a treatment center to prove them wrong. He learned they were right. He also learned that his body couldn't handle the prescription drugs he was taking. He was poisoning himself.

His recovery, says Bishop Varley, is due to "ultimate reliance on Almighty God." But he also cites the "tough love" of those at the center.

Bishop Varley says life has once again become rich for him. "You're free to be the person God intended you to be rather than a slave," he explains.

Are alcohol, pills or anything else enslaving you? Choose life. Seek help. You can do what this courageous clergyman did.

"Blessed is the man who trusts in the Lord, whose trust is the Lord." [JEREMIAH 17:7]

✍ Jesus, turn our lives to reliance on God, not on chemical mood-changers.

Meet Leachim. Leachim is a robot. He teaches in PS 106, Parkchester, New York.

Leachim was created and built for $1,000 as part of an experiment in motivating children to learn. Programmed with seven textbooks and a dictionary, he can handle individual instruction for 50 children, remembering a child by his or her voice in addition to names.

Leachim can even sing a lively rendition of the "Star-Spangled Banner." The third-graders at PS 106 love him. "Leachim should get a medal for being the best teaching machine. Leachim is a regular genius," said one youngster.

Robot teachers may be fun. They may even be good teachers. But a robot can't put a smile on the face of a shy child, or wipe a tear from the eye of a child who has just skinned an elbow.

Only people can do that. It's up to you and me to put that kind of people in our classrooms. That's why better education is everybody's business.

> "Know that we who teach shall be judged with greater strictness." [JAMES 3:1]

 Holy Spirit, inspire young men and women of high ideals and competence to become educators.

Hᴏᴡ ɪs ʏᴏᴜʀ ᴇɴᴇʀɢʏ I.Q.? Columnist Sylvia Porter says recent research gives most Americans a failing grade.

Describing a research project done at Lehman College, she charges that only 30 families out of 600 questioned could answer, "Yes, I am doing this," to all nine questions about their energy-saving efforts. While 74 percent of those questioned were cutting down on air conditioner, TV and auto use, only a third had added house insulation.

More frightening, says Columnist Porter, was the fact that "those who have done the least to shift their lifestyles are families in the higher education—higher income brackets—precisely those who are best informed . . ."

Most of us could uncomplicate our lives a bit. That might mean consuming less energy, skipping an occasional meal or doing without so that others may have. This kind of lifestyle fits in with the Scriptures—and common sense.

> "Do not neglect to do good and to share what you have, for such sacrifices are pleasing to God." [HEBREWS 13:16]

⌇§ Help us to be more cost-conscious, Lord, so that we can avoid being wasteful.

Dᴀᴠɪᴅ Hᴜɢʜᴇs ᴍᴀʏ ʙᴇ the world's only pilot ever shot down by a golf ball.

While flying on a mosquito-spraying mission in California, Mr. Hughes was stunned by a golf ball that shattered his windshield and crashed into his helmet. He instinctively pulled back on the stick, circled until his head cleared, then landed on a small airstrip.

The hard-hit ball had come from a drive down the fairway of the Fort Washington Golf Course. When the ball, with an estimated speed of 175 mph, collided with Mr. Hughes' plane flying at 100 mph, the total impact speed was 275 mph.

He said, after a doctor dug eight fragments from his face, "Two inches to the right and I would have been dead."

The automatic life-saving response of this pilot wasn't accidental. He was trained to react in an emergency. We can be ready when the time comes for us to act fast—if we work at it.

"Commit your work to the Lord, and your plans will be established." [ᴘʀᴏᴠᴇʀʙs 16:3]

৵ Remind us to plan ahead, Lord, for situations in which we have to rely on instant reactions.

Robert Taylor is a millionaire who drives a milk truck.

Mr. Taylor, 41, won his million in the Massachusetts State lottery. Before he began receiving the $50,000 checks each year, he had earned his living driving a milk truck in the Boston suburbs for less than $10,000 a year.

"We were very happy before all this happened to us," said Mr. Taylor, who has three children. Now, he says, "We're not going to let a lot of money spoil that for any of us."

That decision made, Mr. Taylor decided to continue his milk route.

How few people can cope so sanely with sudden success! More often we let it go to our heads where it undermines the values that give our lives joy and meaning.

Enjoy the good that comes your way. But remember to keep first things first.

"If riches increase, set not your heart on them."   [PSALM 62:10]

&ᶘ Jesus, may we lay up treasures where they will last forever.

HAVING NO LEGS DOESN'T keep Melvin Brennis from patching roofs, mowing lawns and hunting.

Run over by a railway log car in 1948, the former switchman lost his legs near the hips. He wouldn't accept a life of inactivity, but determined to keep doing the things he liked to do. He learned to ride, and hunted moose in Canada on horseback. He worked with builders constructing his home in Washington state, made his own cabinets and installed the electric heating. He climbs ladders by pulling himself up by his arms. Recently, he painted a neighbor's roof.

"I never felt sorry for myself," Mr. Brennis, 72, explained. "I just took it from day to day. I never dwell on my difficulties. I'm a happy man."

If we look down the long corridor labeled "future," it can make us dizzy or discouraged. But if we shorten the perspective to one day at a time, things become possible. God strengthens us an instant at a time—and it's a good way to live.

"I can do all things in Him who strengthens me."　　　　　　　[PHILIPPIANS 4:13]

❧ Keep us from getting scared about the future, Holy Spirit.

ONE FASHION ITEM IN AMERICA hasn't changed in 120 years—denim jeans.

Called "Levi's" after their originator, Levi Strauss, the sturdy pants were really an afterthought. A Bavarian immigrant, Mr. Strauss had landed in San Francisco with a roll of canvas intended for tents for the gold rush miners. A miner changed his ideas.

"Should have brought pants," said the miner.

"Pants. Why pants?" asked Mr. Strauss.

"Pants don't wear worth a hoot in the diggin's," said the miner. "Can't get a pair strong enough."

So Levi Strauss made his canvas into pants, bonding their pockets with copper rivets. They were an instant hit.

He later used a tough cotton fabric loomed in Nimes, France, called serge de Nimes. Hence the name "denim."

A chance remark gave Levi Strauss a business, and America what is practically a clothing institution. It highlights the importance of being alert for opportunities. If we're not, we may never even know what we've missed.

> "A man's mind plans his way, but the Lord directs his steps."   [PROVERBS 16:9]

⁝ Holy Spirit, guide us to see God's hand in the events of each day.

BY THE TIME PINO AMATO broke the world hair-cutting record, almost everyone in his hometown of Pavia, Italy, looked freshly barbered.

In a marathon lasting 83 hours, Mr. Amato worked non-stop, cutting the hair of 200 volunteers in four days and three nights. On the fourth night, he finally gave up, suffering from swollen legs and a fever.

Before Mr. Amato's record-breaking feat, the Guinness Book of Records listed Ann Hoy of Brisbane, Australia, as world champion non-stop barber, with 82 hours and 9 minutes of cutting, setting and styling.

Why this drive to excel? What moves people to such extreme exertions? Maybe it's something in people that says: "I'm different from everybody else. In some way, there's nobody like me."

And that's true of each of us. This uniqueness is a gift of God. It has to be discovered, properly understood and put into action.

For most of us, that has nothing to do with record books. It has much to do with how we live.

> "He encircled him, He cared for him, He kept him as the apple of His eye."
> [DEUTERONOMY 32:10]

⋙ Father, You call the stars each by name. Make me aware of how special I am to You.

A MISSING STREET ADDRESS can be fatal, say city officials in Atlanta, Georgia. The director of Atlanta's Bureau of Buildings is conducting a survey of street numbers to insure against that.

"In cardiac cases," says ambulance technician Sam Brantley of Atlanta's Grady Memorial Hospital, "if we don't get to them in four minutes, we've lost them. The same is true in a lot of trauma cases—gunshot wounds and accidents."

The police, too, stress the importance of having street numbers in plain sight, clearly written and away from bushes or signs that might hide them. A minute lost in reaching the scene of a crime can mean tragedy.

A few numbers on a house or a mailbox may seem insignificant—until you realize what can happen if they're not there. Little things do mean a lot. Maybe that's why Jesus said:

"He who is faithful in a very little is faithful also in much."   [LUKE 16:10]

❧ Father, may we give small things the attention they deserve.

A JAIL TURNKEY'S INTEREST changed the life of a Cincinnati, Ohio, derelict and made him $6,000 richer.

John Stone was friendless, broke and without identification when he turned up at the jail looking for shelter for the night. An ex-cook, Mr. Stone was too old to find work and had lost all records of his place or date of birth. But turnkey Al Elsbernd took Mr. Stone's story to reporter John Eliot, whose search turned up the man's birth record in Gallipolis, Ohio. Soon, Mr. Stone received over $6,000 in retroactive Social Security benefits.

"Never thought anybody cared about an old man," he said gratefully. "Now I can get a haircut, a shave, new clothes and some teeth."

Where would our world be if people stopped caring? Not enough do, and that's why so many things are in a mess. But there are a lot of individuals who go around quietly helping friends, relatives and strangers the way Jesus told us to. Their candles can light ours—and ours can do the same for others.

"You are the light of the world."
[MATTHEW 5:14]

❧ Let me see in every person I meet, Lord, someone about whom You care very much.

DO YOU PLAN YOUR DAY, or does it just happen? Some practical tips for getting off to a good start are these by Carolyn Scott, counselor, and Dr. Michael Stadter, psychologist, at Georgetown Psychological Center:

■ Use commuter time to "wind up" and plan your day or to "wind down" and relax after it.

■ Make a list of what must be done, and what you would like to do. Check it off as you go along.

■ Plan a quiet time to relax, re-energize.

■ Build into routine jobs other work you find more satisfying.

■ Take the day a step at a time.

■ Begin your day in the way that best suits you. Either plunge or ease into work.

■ Plan something to look forward to in each day.

Each day passes an instant at a time. We can neither hurry it nor slow its pace. All we can do with time is plan it, use it, squeeze more out of it. Like all God's gifts, treat time with respect.

> "For in God's time all things will be sought
> after." [SIRACH 39:17]

  Make us more time-conscious, Lord, and
  better able to shape the passing seconds for
  good purposes.

OVER 22,000 PEOPLE DIED in Guatemala's earthquake of February, 1976. One million were homeless. Houses, churches, picturesque village squares were reduced to rubble.

The great quake leveled whole towns and villages, particularly in Chimaltenago, a poor, mountainous state. As the roads opened, relief workers noted crudely lettered signs marking paths to isolated communities.

A typical sign read, "The village of San Marcos de Milpas Altas would be grateful to receive blankets, shovels and picks."

A few weeks later, one such message was replaced by a new one, "The village of San Jose del Pino thanks our Brothers and Sisters for the help they have provided us."

Poverty and disaster—here and overseas—aren't faraway impersonal statistics. They are tragic events in human lives. Our love—in action—can help relieve the suffering.

> "Everyone to whom much is given, of him will much be required."   [LUKE 12:48]

      Father, may we put our love of You into action on behalf of our neighbor.

YOUNGSTERS FROM GRADES one through six traded the chrome and plastic desks of Farmington, Maine's modern school system for a day in a one-room school.

As part of National Education Week, 18 different children went each day to a single-room school built in 1854. They sat on hard wooden benches, used a slate and chalk and lunched on bread, cheese, raw carrots, milk and gingerbread.

"This one-room class is pretty good," said one sixth grader. "I like it better than our school, but I think it would be cold here in winter and I wouldn't want to chop the wood for the stove."

It's important to give young people an appreciation of their cultural heritage. Where we've come from has an important bearing on where we're going and what we must do to get there.

But contemporary challenges ultimately demand contemporary solutions. Are you speaking—and working—for a school system that teaches respect for the past and excitement for the future?

> "In your teaching show integrity, gravity and sound speech that cannot be censured."
>
> [TITUS 2:7]

&ß Holy Spirit, guide educators in their work of forming young minds.

IN MURFREESBORO, ARKANSAS, diamonds are free. The town has the only known diamond mine in North America—in one of the most unusual parks in the United States—Crater of Diamonds State Park. For a nominal fee, visitors search the park's surface for diamonds, keeping those they find.

Almost daily, some lucky tourist spots a gem. Over 60,000 have been found on the 78-acre volcanic pile since John Huddleston, a farmer, spied two while plowing in 1906. One gem, the 40.23 carat "Uncle Sam" found in 1925, is considered priceless.

Though Arkansas may eventually mine the site commercially, now there are no shafts, and only the surface is plowed daily. Any stone found becomes the property of the finder, with no taxes unless the gem is sold.

If more of us could look on each day as filled with opportunities instead of trials, diamonds instead of rocks, our actions could change many situations for the better. That's worth thinking about.

> "Lay up your treasure according to the commandments of the Most High, and it will profit you more than gold." [SIRACH 29:11]

Aid us to brighten our outlook, Jesus, so we can improve our performance.

LITTLE LORI BORGES owes her life to 80 mothers. As a baby, Lori suffered from a rare intestinal malfunction. Doctors said she could pull through only if she could live entirely on mother's milk until she was two. She would need at least 60 ounces a day, which would cost $30 a day, a total of $22,000 that Lori's parents didn't have.

Then the Palo Alto, California, Childbirth Education League heard of Lori. Eighty nursing mothers volunteered to give the needed milk, free.

"When I think back over the last few months, I get weepy," says Mrs. Borges. "You almost get the idea these days that people are indifferent. I know this isn't true. I have never met a more beautiful batch of people."

Life. How precious it is. And how promptly most people react when it's threatened. Few can save a life by donating mother's milk. But how about blood? Can you donate blood? If so, will you?

"What shall a man give in return for his life?"   [MATTHEW 16:26]

    Father, make us lovers of life.

OU WOULD PROBABLY be startled if somebody told you: "I'm never going to die." But, according to experts at a meeting sponsored by the American Health Foundation, many people act that way.

At the symposium held in New York, the panelists pointed out that people go back to smoking after heart surgery, they refuse to use seat belts, they eat and drink too much—all in spite of knowledge that such actions court early death.

Armed with the "illusion of immortality," said Dr. Eugene Wynder, "we are able to maintain a life-style which is, in effect, self-destructive."

At the same meeting, Dr. Rollo May, a psychoanalyst, recalled that he was about to put in his place a young intern who told him he was giving up smoking, drinking, coffee and tea because they were having a bad effect on his health. The intern looked at him and shrugged, "It's your life." Those words, said Dr. May, started him thinking.

It is our life and our health, physical and spiritual. Nobody will do much to protect it, if we don't.

"Remember that we all must die."

[SIRACH 8:7]

Keep us from the illusion of immortality, Jesus, and lead us to You as the source of life.

DO YOU PANIC AT figuring a 15 percent tip on a $5.76 lunch bill? Does balancing your checkbook terrify you? If so, you may be a victim of "math anxiety."

Stanley Kogelman and Joseph Warren, two New York math professors, conduct a "Mind Over Math Workshop" to help victims of "math anxiety" overcome their mental blocks. Some participants recall early, emotion-filled school experiences, and find that the "talking cure" works, as it does for other psychological problems.

Soon participants are delighted to discover that they can come up with correct answers to algebra problems. Says Elaine Sorel, a TV-commercial producer who claims she's a star pupil: "The most important thing I got out of the workshops is to trust my own judgment, and not feel like a fool."

Sometimes the hardest person to trust is "me." But if we can slow down, admit our anxiety and try to see the cause, we can usually proceed calmly to a solution. It doesn't mean we'll always be right, but healthy self-confidence will improve our batting average.

> "Keep sound wisdom anl discretion; let them not escape from your sight."
>
> [PROVERBS 3:21]

 ੱ Keep us from panic, Holy Spirit. Lead us step by step to wisdom through Your gentle promptings.

A BOSTON JUDGE CHASED four white youths through city streets after seeing them beat a black man.

Driving in rush hour traffic, Municipal Court Judge Frank Foster, 66, saw attackers beating the man. He leaned on his horn, driving in pursuit when the youths fled. Blocking their flight at a red light, he and police officers took their names. The judge brought the victim and a witness to court and warrants were issued for the four youths' arrest.

"I wanted black people to know there are white people who do care," explained Judge Foster. He was especially concerned, he said, because a similar beating had taken place a day earlier when youths had attacked a 29-year-old black lawyer on the street beneath the mayor's office.

Violence can spark more violence, or it can lead to a constructive response. That's up to you and me. It's your life—and mine. Together we can make a difference.

> "Put away violence and oppression, and execute justice and righteousness."
>
> [EZEKIEL 45:9]

   Instruct us in Your ways, Father, which are so far above our ways. Only with Your help can we learn.

PERHAPS THE TIME is soon coming when Americans will shake their reputation for materialism.

Economist W.E. Hoadley, vice president of Bank of America, predicts:

■ Lower demand for durable goods as Americans see national and personal consumption as wasteful.

■ Fewer purchases of disposable items.

■ Multi-family dwelling units continuing to replace the single-family house.

■ A swing back to thrift and integrity.

One factor in this outlook, reports *Industry Week,* is the increasing percentage of people aged 25 to 34, a group that values quality over quantity, and considers the social implication of their purchases.

Those of us who are still caught up in the habits and social pressures of conspicuous consumption can learn from those with a fresher viewpoint. We can save, and find more contentment.

"Seek first His Kingdom." [MATTHEW 6:33]

&ᎷᎢᎷ Help us, Jesus, to put first things first.

A WOMAN BORN DURING LINCOLN'S lifetime achieved her goal of United States Citizenship in 1975.

Albanian-born Mrika Mrnacaj was 110 when she came to join her sons in the U.S. in 1974. The next year, she took the first step toward becoming a citizen, by applying for permanent residence.

Her expression of love for America moved legislators to submit a bill to Congress to waive the five-year residency and language requirements for her. It was signed by the President in time for the tiny grandmother to be sworn in as a citizen December 30th, 111 years and 6 months after her birth.

"I came here because I want to be with my sons and be American like them," she told reporters. "There is no other country like this. I came to die—and to live—in a free country."

Sometimes citizens lose sight of the values in our country that new immigrants are quick to see. Sure, there are things wrong with America. But there's a lot of good, too. What are we doing to make it better?

"Righteousness exalts a nation."
[PROVERBS 14:34]

&ε Give us a deeper appreciation of our country, Father, as well as a respect for those of others.

Some of the world's saddest people may be professional comedians, says Dr. Samuel Janus, a New York psychologist, who has studied the comic personality.

Offstage, he claims, most comedians are depressed, anxious and fearful. Making jokes is their defense against a hostile world.

"Many of our top comedians, if one listens to their routines, are really crying out loud," says Dr. Janus. His research with 55 top comics shows that most come from humble backgrounds and struggled against severe childhood traumas.

But, he concludes, comedians "are not really sickies. They're really very sweet, sensitive guys. Most are very stable people, good family men."

This insight into comedians reinforces the fact that to be depressed and fearful—at least some times—is nothing abnormal. Such feelings can be put to constructive use. And you don't have to be a comedian to bring a smile to the lips of others.

> "Anxiety in a man's heart weighs him down,
> but a good word makes him glad."
> [PROVERBS 12:25]

    es Jesus, make us able to turn our discomforts into a source of comfort for our neighbors.

Mother Teresa of Calcutta and her Missionaries of Charity help the unwanted dying—the "poorest of the poor" in India.

In his book, *Something Beautiful for God,* Malcolm Muggeridge, the English journalist, quotes Mother Teresa:

"In these twenty years of work among the people," she said, "I have come to realize that being unwanted is the worst disease that any human being can ever experience . . .

"For all kinds of disease there are medicines and cures. But for being unwanted, except there are willing hands to serve and there's a loving heart to love, I don't think this terrible disease can ever be cured."

It's not just those dying in the streets in India who feel unwanted. Look around. Could you make the difference for someone who has no one to care?

"Hold fast to what is good; love one another with brotherly affection." [ROMANS 12:9,10]

✤ Help me, Father, to love my brothers and sisters as Your Son taught us to love.

Teaching kindergarten is a man's work, Bernie Hanlon believes. And he's proving it.

Mr. Hanlon, 27, teaches kindergarten in Cypress, California. He surprised former students, other teachers and pre-schoolers' parents by deciding to "be demoted." And he's happy with it. A 6-foot-1 athletic type, he often walks around the classroom on his knees, and delights youngsters with his imaginative and fatherly approach.

"People seem to think that men don't have what it takes to be close to little children," he says. "One of the problems kids have is that they are surrounded by women. There is a desperate need for some male images. I feel I'm better for the experience. It's taught me how to have more patience and more understanding for the smaller child."

Students need more teachers—men and women—who will approach them with understanding. And teachers need encouragement from parents. One way to better schools is to build up a spirit of mutual support.

"One with much experience will speak with understanding."   [SIRACH 34:9]

❧ Make us more interested in education, Lord, and in guiding youngsters.

Martha Drane told her children, before she died in 1948, that they would eventually inherit "some money" from their father whom she had left some years before. They thought it was a pipedream.

With the aid of a 125-year-old Bible, the pipedream became reality seven years after Ben Drane died in Nashville, Tennessee, at the age of 100.

His lawyer finally gave investigators, Ben Jones and J.R. Jones, the job of combing the country for the family. As the search narrowed, they confirmed identities with the aid of the recorded names and birthdates in a Bible owned by members of the family found in Oklahoma.

Ben Drane had left $1.5 million. "I'll bet they can use the money," said Ben Jones. "I wouldn't describe any of them as real poor but they aren't rich either, until now, that is."

The custom of listing family names in a Bible is testimony to the continuity of belief. Is faith an open book or a closed one in your family?

> "Now faith is the assurance of things hoped
> for, the conviction of things not seen."
> [HEBREWS 11:1]

ᨦ Let Your word be a living and vital reality in our home, Jesus.

WANT TO LEARN TO WRITE? These tongue-in-cheek "rules for good riting" may (or may not) help:

- Each pronoun agrees with their antecedent.
- Verbs has to agree with their subjects.
- Don't use no double negatives.
- When dangling, don't use participles.
- A writer mustn't shift your point of view. .
- Check to see if you any words out.
- Don't abbrev.
- Don't use commas, which aren't necessary.
- Just between you and I, case is important.
- Join clauses good, like a conjunction should.
- Don't use a run-on sentence you got to punctuate

it.

- About sentence fragments.
- Last but not least, lay off the cliches.

The message comes first in any communication. But things like neatness, language, courtesy and spelling count, too. Don't let carelessness stifle your efforts to convey God's truth.

> "For this I was born, and for this I have come into the world, to bear witness to the truth." [JOHN 18:37]

    Jesus, You communicated God's love effectively. May we do the same.

To TEENAGE GIRLS, careers are a top priority, according to a Y.W.C.A. survey.

In a sampling of 1,112 girls from El Paso, Texas; Greenville, South Carolina; Philadelphia; and South Bend, Indiana; job training took first place in every group. Typical teen comments on the questionnaires were these:

"We need training for a wider variety of jobs."

"Why aren't girls trained to do anything outside the house besides office work?"

"Girls usually don't get any training except for secretarial or teaching jobs."

We've come a long way from the days when steno and typing were the only job skills girls were offered. A long way, but not far enough.

How about your home, your school, your office? Are women and girls "second-class citizens" there?

"Do not withhold good from those to whom it is due, when it is in your power to do it."
[PROVERBS 3:27]

  Holy Spirit, show us ways to increase equal opportunity for all.

A VOLUNTEER SQUAD of 300 California Bay Area residents are resettling 400 animals a month.

The "refugees" are sick, injured or orphaned wilderness creatures. The rescuers are working with the Bay Area Wildlife Rehabilitation Council.

Baby birds, orphaned fawns, squirrels, brush rabbits, gophers, raccoons and opossums are treated and released in the wilds by the unpaid volunteers.

"Every now and then someone tells me I'm wasting my time breaking my neck over a raccoon or a sea gull because they're not endangered," says one worker. "We just don't weigh the value of a life by the rarity of the species. Even if I would tolerate that attitude—which I won't—my volunteers wouldn't."

Vegetable, animal and human lives are locked in a delicate balance by the Creator. If we become hardened to the plight of any, we threaten—at least a little —all. Are you a lover of earth?

> "Ever since the creation of the world, His invisible nature has been clearly perceived in the things that have been made."
>
> [ROMANS 1:20]

   ~&#127; Father, may our acts show our gratitude for the riches of creation.

Two CONNECTICUT GOVERNMENT officials and 250 other people spent a day working in wheel chairs to dramatize the problems of the handicapped.

The limitations Lieutenant Governor Robert Killian and Secretary of State Gloria Schaffer experienced were part of "Awareness Day".

Mr. Killian and Mrs. Schaffer found many obstacles in their own offices—doorways too narrow, phones and drinking fountains out of reach, ramps too steep. "I really felt I was a handicapped person," Mrs. Schaffer said afterward. Lieutenant Governor Killian, unable to mount the dais, made a moving speech from a table on the chamber floor in support of a bill to require new housing facilities for the handicapped.

Once you become conscious of obstacles, you begin to find them nearly everywhere.

Could we do more to remind public officials to make provision for the handicapped? Sometimes their biggest handicap is our indifference.

"Give Your servant therefore an understanding mind."   [1 KINGS 3:9]

Increase our sensitivity, Jesus, to the requirements of other persons.

FEW RETIREES have 65-year-old Dorothea Thorsen's hobby. She is an accomplished mountain climber.

"I may be 65 years old but on the trail I'm 49," says Mrs. Thorsen, who has scaled Arizona's 9,432-foot Mt. Wrightstown 87 times, and aims at 100.

A local celebrity in Tucson, Arizona, because of her climbing, Mrs. Thorsen has conquered 116 mountains since she began at age 8. Many she has scaled 40 or 50 times. To keep in shape, she bicycles and swims.

How long will she keep climbing? Mrs. Thorsen cites an uncle of hers who just gave up mountain climbing—at age 88. "But," she adds, "he still hikes 25 to 35 miles a week."

Just reading about such activities is enough to cause shortness of breath in some of us. While this is an extreme example, there is a fascination about climbing mountains. Is it just exercise? The desire to set records? The effort to gain perspective on life? To get beyond the limitations of earth? To seek the divine?

> "Come, let us go up to the mountain of the Lord . . . that He may teach us His ways."
> [ISAIAH 2:3]

૭క్ When we seek Your help, Father, hear us!

O VER 10,000 PEOPLE WELCOMED the 60-foot sailing canoe *Hokuléa* after its 2,400-mile voyage from Hawaii to Tahiti. Its arrival day was declared a Tahitian holiday.

A Bicentennial project of the state of Hawaii, the canoe voyage was designed to show that ancient Polynesians could have sailed the Pacific guided only by the stars. The 15-man crew sailed without any modern navigation equipment, though a radio was aboard and an escort vessel sailed nearby.

The trip tested a theory that 1,000 years ago Polynesians migrated across the Pacific to Hawaii or in the opposite direction, for trade.

Our nation's Bicentennial did much to bring a fragmented and wounded people together again. In our daily lives, we can continue that spirit of harmony and goodwill.

Let's not wait another 200 years before carrying the Founders' dream to fulfillment.

"Behold, how good and pleasant it is when brothers dwell in unity!"   [PSALM 133:1]

❧ Father, make us more deeply one people.

AMERICAN BUSINESS appears to be responding to the challenge of consumerism. The Harvard Business Review, in a poll of 3,418 corporate executives, found most in agreement that "consumerism is both good for business and for the consumer."

Consumerism may be described as the effort to equalize the rights, access to information and power of the buyer with those of the seller.

Some positive examples:

■ Seven-Up developed a plastic bottle, degradable in solid waste treatment.

■ Sears put out a phosphate-free detergent.

■ General Motors introduced a "service superiority" program for dealers that has led to a big drop in complaints.

■ Kodak started a policy of anticipating customer mistakes and "designing them out" of the product.

If you buy a defective product, you owe it to yourself and other consumers to seek redress. But, remember, consumers have a responsibility to be honest too.

> "Buy truth and do not sell it; buy wisdom, instruction, and understanding."
> [PROVERBS 23:23]

    ✒ Make me more aware of my duty to be honest and truthful in all my dealings, Lord.

A BLIND MECHANIC? It's not as bizarre as you might think.

John DiBattiste of Hubbard, Ohio, can tell what's the matter with a car just by listening. He doesn't have to check under the hood.

Blind for the past eight years, Mr. DiBattiste confines his efforts to helping neighbors and relatives. He isn't a licensed mechanic. But he has done brake jobs, replaced water pumps, installed exhaust systems and replaced shock absorbers.

Once the sightless handyman worked on electrical wiring in his own home. "I got knocked right on my you-know-what," he laughed. "But I love electrical work so much it hasn't scared me off!"

People who love their work usually do better work. They are always searching for ways to improve. That is good for them and for the people served by their efforts.

Useful work, engaged in wholeheartedly, can be seen as a continuation of God's work of creation.

"Whatever your task, work heartily."
[COLOSSIANS 3:23]

  Make us more attentive to our jobs, Lord, to do them better for ourselves and others.

WHAT NEEDS TO BE DONE if the world is to feed itself adequately? These points emerged from a meeting of 24 livestock and food experts:

■ Cattle can be fed on alternative feeds, such as municipal waste, the discard of wood pulp, the by-products of slaughterhouses and juices from the pulp of apples and oranges.

■ By 1985, the world's underdeveloped countries will be producing 76 million tons less grain each year than they will need.

■ The United States needs a national food policy that will take into account the feeding of hungry peoples as well as protection of local industries.

■ Rangeland—40 percent of the world's land area—could support two or three times more cattle than it does now.

For the foreseeable future, people will be living on the verge of famine. There are no easy formulas. Long-range and short-term solutions are needed. The Lord of all expects us to care about those in distress.

> "Lord, when did we see You hungry and feed You, or thirsty and give You drink?"
> [MATTHEW 25:37]

&⸹ Jesus, make us more conscious of our brothers and sisters who don't have enough to eat.

BOB CONSIDINE, NEWSPAPERMAN, columnist and author of 25 books, was a deeply religious man. His "Newspaperman's Prayer" Reflects His Faith:

"Dear God, may I be fair. Circumstances and dumb luck have placed in my thumby paws a degree of authority which I may not fully comprehend. Let me not profane it.

"Never let me slip into writing DOWN, in fatuous fear that readers will not understand. Let me write from the shoulder, and always with the assumption that those who read know more than I.

"Let me use my legs and eyes, the better to track down and see the truth. When the customers write in to accuse me of being a bum, let me consider carefully the possibility that I am . . . and try to do better. Let me work harder, try harder and recall with proper humility that history produced some notably abler reporters, including four journeymen named Matthew, Mark, Luke and John."

To which, all one can say is: Amen.

"And every work that he undertook . . . seeking his God, he did with all his heart."
[2 CHRONICLES 31:20]

Successful retirement needs 10 years of planning, says Max Roffman, who teaches a unique "retirement course" at the University of Hawaii.

Mr. Roffman, a 66-year-old former labor leader, based the course on his own experiences.

"So many people face retirement . . ." he says. "They think only in terms of money. Without planning, the other problems can be a traumatic shock."

To lessen the shock, Mr. Roffman deals with hobbies, health, budgeting, wills, and consumer problems. Throughout, he stresses that "there is no age at which people aren't able to enjoy themselves. The important thing is for the elderly to take an interest in life around them."

A balanced life involves commitment to the present and prudent planning for the future. If we get on well with the people and circumstances around us, there's no reason to fear the dawn of tomorrow. As we live, so shall we retire.

"Let not your heart faint, and be not fearful."   [JEREMIAH 51:46]

&es; God, You are the source of our hope and life.

A TEENAGER'S DREAM of creating a cathedral window became a reality—35 years later.

When Rowan LeCompte first visited Washington's National Cathedral at age 14, he decided he wanted to design a rose window for the famous church.

Ever since, Mr. LeCompte studied and worked. Largely self-trained, he created 20 other stained glass windows for the cathedral before finally completing the giant rose window—almost 26 feet in diameter.

"It's a celebrative window," Mr. LeCompte says. "A song of praise to the universe." The 51-year-old artist regards the window as his masterpiece.

Our "song of praise" can take many forms—the grateful memories of family or friends, a life of cheerful service, an attitude of listening and helping.

In ways like these, the light of God's love can shine through us.

> "This is how one should regard us, as servants of Christ and stewards."
>
> [1 CORINTHIANS 4:1]

~§ Make us more conscious, Jesus, of how we can reflect the divine concern for humanity.

RESEARCH STUDENTS AT TEXAS TECH University have "an owl who came in from the cold."

Proving his legendary wisdom, the West Texas ground owl began staying near the university's research center as the weather got colder. Students grew familiar with the studious looking bird, greeting him with a "Hello, Owl" as they came and went, until a fierce norther sent the mercury dipping.

Owl made his move, slipping into the research building to make his home among the warm pipes and machinery. His student friends adopted him.

Fish, fowl and four-footed creatures have a built-in drive to seek what is good for them. So do we. But, free to choose, we can often make the wrong choice—usually out of fear, selfishness or a desire for short-term gain.

In matters of consequence, take the long view. Include God and neighbor. That way, you'll never be left out in the cold.

"Let us choose what is right." [JOB 34:4]

⋙ Father, in our decisions teach us to seek Your will.

WHEN COUNTRY-WESTERN COMPOSER Walter Gaskins tries out his songs, he really has a captive audience. He's sheriff at a county jail.

"They seem to get quite a kick out of it," says Sheriff Gaskins of the County Jail in Nashville, Georgia.

His most popular song is "The Ballad of Lamar Fountain," dedicated to one of his prisoners.

What kind of man sings songs to his prisoners? This man has never carried a gun. "I've always been able to talk my way out of things most of the time," he said. "There's not many people who'll shoot you unless they feel that they're going to get shot."

As for the songs, he feels they help some of the prisoners. "If I can help just one out of 100," he says, "I'm doing good."

The sheriff sings songs. Each of us has something to offer wherever we are. It could be leadership, creativity, organizational ability—encouragement, understanding, a song or a smile. The point is, you can make a difference.

"I will sing with the spirit and I will sing with the mind also."   [1 CORINTHIANS 14:15]

⁓ Lord, may we never underestimate our ability to make the world a little better for someone.

A 1,600-MILE BICYCLE TRIP from New Orleans to Chicago was one family's contribution to a fund-raising campaign for St. Jude's Children's Hospital. At the 38-day trip's end, Darryl and Carol Levesque delivered a $1 million check for St. Jude's, from Epsilon Sigma Alpha Women's International, a service organization to which Carol belongs.

"We had no problems with the motorists but a few thunderstorms in Kentucky slowed us down," said Darryl. He and Carol rode a 9½-foot bicycle built for four, with seats for their daughters, Michelle, 4, and Andrea, 2.

"We stopped for a tour of the hospital (St. Jude's)," Carol Levesque related. "I looked at the faces of the kids there and then at Michelle and Andrea. It's all the motivation you need to keep on going."

The thought that somebody needs what we have to give can keep us going a long time. Having a purpose is half the secret in life. The other half is putting that purpose into gear.

> "Decide on a matter, and it will be established for you, and light will shine on your ways."   [JOB 22:28]

    ✥ Sometimes I feel I'm going nowhere, Lord. Help me find a direction and a reason to reach out.

HAT'S IN A WORD? Cartoonist Jules Feiffer put these comments into the mouth of one of his characters:

"I used to think I was poor.

Then they told me I wasn't poor, I was needy.

Then they told me it was self-defeating to think of myself as needy, I was deprived.

Then they told me deprived was a bad image. I was underprivileged.

Then they told me underprivileged was overused, I was disadvantaged.

I still don't have a dime, but I have a great vocabulary."

Remember the War on Poverty? It had some solid accomplishments. But, as an expression of government bureaucracy, it often dealt more in words than actions, more in terminology than in reality.

Maybe the war wasn't won because not enough experts consulted those most affected—poor people themselves. Giving people control over their own destinies is a good way to start change.

"A just man knows the rights of the poor."
[PROVERBS 29:7]

Help us remember, Father, that great good can be accomplished only through effort.

JOHN COLLINS HAS THE world's rarest profession—for a man. When Mr. Collins received his Master's degree from Yale, he became the only male midwife in the United States.

As a midwife, he can, under a doctor's supervision, treat a woman with a normal pregnancy, deliver her child and teach both parents to care for it.

"Until a few years ago colleges wouldn't let men train in maternal nursing," said Mr. Collins, "but now the field is more open." He sees being a male as an advantage in involving the husband and wife together in the process of preparing for and caring for a child.

Each of us has some opportunity—and obligation—to preserve and nurture human life. Life is threatened in many areas—on the battlefield, on the streets, in prison, in the womb, even in the home. Do what you can to stand up for God's most basic gift.

> "His divine power has granted to us all things that pertain to life." [2 PETER 1:3]

◄§ Make us more conscious, Lord, of Your support as we try to defend life in all its stages.

OREST JOWYK, 9, of Douglaston, New York, hated gym. Born with dislocated hips and chronic bronchitis, he could barely walk. The other kids made fun of him in gym class.

One doctor suggested ballet as therapy. But Orest hated that, too. Then his parents thought of ice skating. "He got around the rink with help," his mother recalls. "He was happy and smiling."

Today, Orest Jowyk is 15 and he's still smiling. He's North Atlantic Junior Men's Figure Skating champion, with hopes for the next Olympics.

He practices six hours a day—even in summertime. "I don't mind," he says. "Nobody laughs anymore."

Orest and his parents could have given up when he was nine, leaving him an invalid. Instead, they kept on looking for a constructive solution. We can give up. Or we can keep on. Perseverance may not be easy. But giving up gets us nowhere.

> "Be strong and of good courage . . . He will not fail you or forsake you."
> [DEUTERONOMY 31:6]

₱ Holy Spirit, help us to keep on going when our spirits flag.

WHAT DO YOU GET WHEN YOU MIX garlic juice, food scraps, cow manure and electrodes?

Harry Pfau of Citrus Springs, Florida, gets 3½-lb. tomatoes, 4-lb. radishes and pole beans three feet high.

Mr. Pfau, who grows the gigantic vegetables in a retirement community, spreads his aged compost of kitchen scraps over the soil, then runs strings of copper wire between poles at the garden's edge. He runs insulated bell wires from them to the plant roots, to conduct atmospheric changes into the soil.

Once the plants begin to grow, Mr. Pfau sprinkles them with a garlic juice solution to kill bugs.

Does science back Mr. Pfau's eccentric methods?

"It's never been proven," he concedes, "but it's never been disproved either. And I have seen it happen with my own eyes."

Many scientific breakthroughs occur because one person labored hard and creatively without watching the clock. That's worth thinking about.

> "The work of a man's hand comes back to him." [PROVERBS 12:14]

✒ Remind us when we need it, Holy Spirit, that creative thinking requires willingness to work hard.

Davıd Cunnıngham, 88, is a retired janitor living in Columbus, Ohio. But he never stopped doing his life's main work.

Mr. Cunningham had a conversion experience in 1921 and turned his attention to helping youth. "It seemed children were so neglected," he said. "I started teaching them Bible verses, how the 12 men that followed Jesus wanted disciples too."

From this came invitations for "Brother Dave" to teach Sunday School classes over a wide area.

At his home, children are always welcome. They get candy, conversation and stories. And they put together newsletters to send to old persons and shut-ins.

The local Church of God repeatedly asked Mr. Cunningham to be its pastor. "But the Lord didn't call me to be a pastor," he smiled. "He called me for the children."

And the Kingdom of God is made up of those who become like little children.

> "Unless you turn and become like children you will never enter the kingdom of heaven."
> [MATTHEW 18:3]

⋐ঠ Remind us, Jesus, of the attitudes we need to enter Your kingdom.

ARITAL SPATS can be a good thing, says Dr. M. J. Bienvenu of Louisiana's Northwestern State University. But he lays down these important rules of "combat":

- Stick to the issue. Don't revive old hurts.
- Don't attack each other as persons.
- Don't use words to kill, but to dig out what's bothering each person deep down—to release tensions.
- Get feelings out before you lose control, when both of you have the time and privacy.
- Really try to look at the issue from the other's point of view.
- Build a climate of "safety of expression," trusting each other and treating shared feelings as "privileged communications."

No serious relationship can be all sweetness and light. But few can survive a determined effort by either party to win at all costs. That's not winning, but losing. The friendship dies.

If we really care, even when we're mad we'll stick to facts and feelings—and not call names.

> "Let all bitterness and wrath and anger and clamor and slander be put away from you."
> [EPHESIANS 4:31]

  ₰   Give us a sense of fairness and objectivity, Father, especially when we are under great pressure.

T HE SKILL OF MANAGING isn't automatically inherited with a job promotion. It comes, says *Supervisory
Management Magazine,* from doing your job in the
following ways:

■ Be willing to pay the price for what you want.
■ Learn to accept responsibility.
■ Learn to accept help from others.
■ Spend your time on the really important things.
■ Express your feelings; understand others' feelings.
■ Establish and maintain good relations with others.
■ Face problems in terms of the present, not the
past or the future.
■ Appraise your own performance honestly.
■ Before attempting to manage others, be able to
manage yourself.

We all have things to manage, at home and on the
job. If we use wisely the brains God gave us, we'll get
more done, with less spinning of wheels, than we might
have thought possible. And that's good management.

"Gird up your minds."   [1 PETER 1:13]

◆⟡ Remind us to stop and think, Jesus, before
we start doing things.

I**F YOU WERE DEAF**, how would you carry on an emergency telephone conversation? A county policeman in Atlanta, Georgia, found one way.

Frustrated by an experience of vainly trying to give directions to a deaf couple, Patrolman J. F. Keenan enrolled in a sign language course at a school for the deaf. There he learned about a teletype communications system used by the deaf to communicate via telephone lines.

Patrolman Keenan persuaded his chief to install the system at police headquarters. Installation in a deaf person's home costs about $200.

It's slower than an ordinary telephone conversation, says Chief Francis D. Hand, "but it's faster than not getting it at all."

Efforts to enable the deaf to communicate seem laborious. Perhaps this very difficulty can lead us to take our verbal faculty less for granted. We hear the words, but do we get the message. Do we really listen?

"Hear the commandments of life . . . Give ear, and learn wisdom." [BARUCH 3:9]

ھۇ We thank You, Father, for our speech and hearing. May we use them to reach out in love.

A DISABLED WIDOW IN HILLSDALE, Michigan, nearly lost her faith in human goodness—but her neighbors more than renewed it for her.

When 51-year-old Georgia McCloe came home from the hospital, she found that a thief had drained 250 gallons of oil from her furnace tank. Mrs. McCloe, who had suffered five strokes, had little income outside her social security check.

Then her neighbors heard of her loss, and chipped in $120 for her fuel bill. When that was gone, Mrs. McCloe didn't have trouble heating her home. A retired banker offered to keep her tank filled throughout the winter.

Government assistance programs are needed. But so is a greater sense of neighborliness.

The best way to have a friend is to be a friend. Does one of your neighbors need something you can supply? Your time? Your help in shopping? A loan? A smile? Why not give it and make two people richer?

> "Do good to a friend before you die, and reach out and give him as much as you can." [SIRACH 14:13]

⊷ Remind us that we were put here on earth, Lord, to develop ourselves by serving others.

IF YOU READ AT AVERAGE freshman high school level, income tax forms, the Bible and directions for TV dinners may be too difficult to understand.

So claims professor Ted Kilty of Western Michigan University, who recently measured readability of everyday writing.

Professor Kilty's study used a standard formula that rates readability by the amount of education it takes to read and understand a given piece of writing. He rated this year's federal tax forms at 9.3 (ninth grade, third month)—the same level as the 23rd Psalm in the King James Version Bible.

Other readability levels Professor Kilty found include: directions on one aspirin brand, 10.3; life insurance policies, 12.7; one frozen turkey dinner, 10.3.

A lot of people in our country can't read well. A lot more find reading a bore. I wish it were otherwise. Maybe each of us could try to encourage another person to read a thoughtful book, magazine or newspaper.

> "Iron sharpens iron, and one man sharpens another."   [PROVERBS 27:17]

     Help us to improve ourselves, Lord, in every way we can.

WHAT IS THE BEST DEFENSE against muggers? Fainting, says a former mugger with 10 years experience.

The ex-mugger and six other former purse-snatchers and con-artists met with police and 200 elderly men and women at New York's John Jay College to talk about self-defense.

"A mugger's not thinking about hurting anybody," explained the reformed thug. "He's just thinking about getting the money. So you gotta throw him off. Faint. Go limp. Act like you're having a seizure or a heart attack. The guy will panic. And you're O.K."

All the former muggers and police agreed on one thing: Don't struggle with a mugger. Don't do anything to anger him.

Said one elderly woman who lives alone, "I think this will help me keep my wits better."

Crime is so widespread in our society that every bit of advice that can slow it down deserves a hearing. Do all you can, together with other citizens and police, to make your neighborhood safer.

> "Do justice and righteousness, and deliver from the hand of the oppressor him who has been robbed." [JEREMIAH 22:3]

> ◆§ Help us take responsibility, Lord, for people and property in the area in which we live.

FEELING NERVOUS? TENSE? Take a walk instead of a tranquilizer, says Herbert de Vries.

Dr. de Vries is an exercise physiologist at the University of Southern California. And he has found that 15 minutes of exercise is better than a tranquilizer pill in easing stress.

Dr. de Vries feels that his findings are especially valuable for older people, whose reactions can be dangerously slowed by tranquilizers.

Moderate exercise not only calms nervous tension, he claims, but it also improves body tone and brings a general feeling of well-being.

No one should undertake a prolonged or strenuous exercise program without careful preparation and a doctor's guidance. But no one should sit around and vegetate either.

The ancient Romans had a saying: "A healthy mind in a healthy body." It's a bit of wisdom that merits serious consideration by anyone who wants the energy to change the world for the better.

> "There is no wealth better than health of body." [SIRACH 30:16]

᠅ Holy Spirit, give us the wisdom to balance work, play and rest in our lives.

ABANDONED FOR 30 YEARS, a 150-year-old stone church has been resurrected as a "labor of love" by townspeople of Milton, New York.

The historic First Baptist Church, built in 1826, had been gradually falling into decay when Milton's citizens decided that "something had to be done." Engineers, carpenters, housewives and businessmen pitched in to clear away underbrush, reinforce floors, replace two chimneys and install electrical wiring. Most work was done on a volunteer basis, but five church members signed a $5,000 note to finance paint and materials.

Two months after the volunteers began, services were held in the church, exactly 182 years after the first congregation had met in an earlier wooden building.

A common need can bring people together and help them understand each other. Repairing a local landmark, like a church, is one place to start.

The personal bond that working together can produce may have far-reaching consequences. The spirit gives life to the deed.

"My Spirit abides among you; fear not."
[HAGGAI 2:5]

ॐ Sharpen our perception, Holy Spirit, so we can see what needs to be done and do it.

John Murray of Stornway, Outer Hebrides, is in love with the Gaelic he learned as a child.

And he has decided to try to preserve Gaelic as the daily language of the 32,000 inhabitants of the Outer Hebrides. It is not spoken there, but merely studied as a school subject—like "Latin."

Mr. Murray hopes to stop the inroads English is making on the widespread use of the ancient tongue.

"Gaelic isn't something you do in your spare time," he explains. "It's a whole world. The sea roars in Gaelic. The birds sing in Gaelic. The dogs bark in Gaelic."

Today, we are becoming more aware of the value of ethnic distinctions. We are exploring our roots more deeply, and coming to respect the differences we see in others.

One way to follow Christ is to be open to everybody. Together, we make up the beautiful blend that is the family of God our Father.

"The Lord gave me a tongue as my reward, and I will praise Him with it." [SIRACH 1:22]

    Make us more respectful of language, Holy Spirit, because it is our chief means of communication.

ONE RECENT SPRING, the season of campus capers, 700 students at Indiana University of Pennsylvania fasted for 30 hours. Their goal was to raise $5,000 for people who "live" with starvation.

The Newman Center's World Hunger Committee started with $205.48 in the bank. With the help of friends and relatives, money and pledges started to pour in. The total reached $11,000.

The cost of the campaign was only two percent. Six thousand dollars went to an organization called Bread for the World. The rest went to seven relief agencies.

All of us, young and old, could do more to alleviate human need. We respond when the challenge is presented in a persuasive way. As we reach out with compassion, we can focus our energies and grow in important ways.

Everybody gains when people band together to lessen the sum total of the world's suffering.

"If one member suffers, all suffer together."
[1 CORINTHIANS 12:26]

੭ৎ Guide us, Lord, in facing challenges that will help us to grow by serving others.

A CASUAL CHAT WITH AN OLD FRIEND changed Anna Clauda from a clerk-typist to a welder.

Ms. Clauda, a 29-year-old woman in Flushing, New York, was locked into a clerical job, supporting her 8-year-old son on $115 a week, when she saw her friend Eddie Kaspshak welding an iron fence.

"It was like fate," she says. "I stopped to say hello. I kept on watching what he was doing. It really looked interesting."

Says Mr. Kaspshak, "I told her 'O.K., you think you can do it; do it.' " A few days later, Ms. Clauda became an apprentice at the welding firm.

"The guys have been wonderful," she says. "This is a very lucky opportunity for me. I make $7.50 an hour. And here, I'm not chained to a typewriter. Every job we do is different."

Being a welder is not for everybody, male or female. But it is an option. Do the changing roles associated with the women's movement interest or repel you? Either way, it's worth the effort to ask "why?"

"Do not find fault before you investigate."
[SIRACH 11:7]

Deepen our desire to study changing circumstances, Lord, before deciding for or against them.

Psychologist Donald T. Campbell believes that morals are due for a comeback.

Dr. Campbell, president of the American Psychological Association, spoke out against the trend of modern psychologies as "individualistically hedonistic, explaining all human behavior in terms of individual pleasure and pain, individual needs and drives."

Such commandments as "Love thy neighbor" and "Honor thy parents" are not just quaint religious and moral traditions, Dr. Campbell argues, but scientifically valid. He urged his listeners to revise their teaching of the young so as not to give the impression "that psychology's current beliefs are the final truth on these matters." He also suggested that the religious objections to some school textbooks may be right.

Experience teaches that there is more to life than pleasure and pain. There is caring. This quality is always in short supply.

When we show love for our neighbors, we are a step closer to the kind of world God intended for us all.

"Beloved, let us love one another; for love is of God, and he who loves is born of God and knows God." [1 JOHN 4:7]

≈§ Help us, Jesus, to show love in our relationships with others.

IN THE SAN FRANCISCO AREA, 2,000 volunteers are helping prisoners to avoid the revolving door of release and return.

A journalist, for example, makes monthly visits to Dick, 27, convicted of attempted rape and sent to prison for three years.

Dick will be on parole soon. The journalist has two job possibilities lined up and will spend his first free day with Dick.

When his friend first came to see him, Dick asked why.

"I told him I believe in God," says the visitor. ". . . we are our brother's keepers and I feel responsible for more than just myself and my family . . . relating with him would do him good maybe and for sure it would me."

"Am I my brother's keeper?"—one of the first questions in the Bible. Today more and more are answering "yes" by constructive action. Why not be one?

"He who loves his brother abides in the light, and in it there is no cause for stumbling." [1 JOHN 2:10]

᧞ Father, help us to love one another.

"I'M KIND OF ANXIOUS to meet God," said an active 81-year-old doctor. "I've got a lot of questions about the human body that I want to ask Him."

"It's good to be a doctor," says Dr. Constantine L. A. Oden of Muskegon, Michigan. "I like people and like to relieve them of anxieties and pains . . ." He has hobbies, too: photography, astronomy, music and cartooning. Large photographs, some of them award winners, line the walls of his office.

The doctor relishes each day, the new things he learns, the fresh problems to solve. "I like my whole life," says Dr. Oden, "I love my family and my friends. I live well because I have my health." Asked when he will retire, he looks at his steady hands, and says when they get shaky he'll quit.

This doctor's prescription for a productive life seems to be equal parts of faith in a God who has answers, hope for each new day and a genuine love for people. It sounds like good medicine for any of us.

"So faith, hope and love abide, these three."
[1 CORINTHIANS 13:13]

Jesus, help us to build our lives on the message You gave us.

Holy Thursday speaks to men across the centuries in accents that are muted with sadness yet tinged with the first glimmers of hope.

St. Luke's Gospel provides us with many lessons from the events of the day. To cite but a few:

1. The need for prayer—As Jesus prayed in the garden, "His sweat became like great drops of blood falling down upon the ground." Coming upon His disciples sleeping, He told them: "Rise and pray that you may not enter into temptation." (22:44-46)

2. The power of forgiveness—When one of those who were leading Jesus away had his right ear cut off by a disciple, "He touched his ear and healed him." (22:51)

3. The example of service—At the Last Supper, Jesus told His followers: "The kings of the Gentiles exercise lordship over them; and those in authority over them are called benefactors. But not so with you; rather let the greatest among you become as the youngest, and the leader as one who serves . . . I am among you as one who serves." (22:25-27)

  § Let my life proclaim by deeds of loving service to others, Lord, that I am Your disciple.

RAGGED CLOAK on His shoulders
a crown of thorns on His head—
"Here is the Man!"
Whipped and mocked and falsely charged
"Here is the man!"
Abandoned by His friends
Cast off by His people—
"Here is the Man!"
Look at the loser, the victim, the scapegoat.
He has no armies, no advocates, scarcely a friend.
"Here is the Man!"
Alone—yet not lonely.
Beaten—yet undefeated.
Crushed—yet calm.
"Here is the Man!"
And in that one Man, see all men.
In His defeat was born our victory.
"Here is the Man!"

"By His great mercy we have been born
anew to a living hope through the resurrec-
tion of Jesus Christ."   [1 PETER 1:3]

ONE FRIDAY, A LETTER ARRIVED for 20-year-old Louis Pucci in East Harlem. It was from a woman thanking him for putting on her windshield the license number of a car which had struck her parked auto.

It wasn't the first time the young man had gotten involved. Some months before, he had accompanied home a woman who was nervous because three men had been watching her. Both were attacked and Louis was stabbed. He recovered.

On Thursday, the day before the driver's letter arrived, Louis Pucci noticed a group of boys outside a grocery store. The owner was his friend, and Louis when in to warn him. When he came out, the gang confronted him, and one of them shot him in the neck. He died without ever seeing the thank-you note.

Caring about our neighbor doesn't always involve risking death. But it can. Is it worth it? Think of the sort of world we'd have if nobody cared.

"Love bears all things, believes all things, hopes all things, endures all things. Love never ends."   [1 CORINTHIANS 13:7,8]

∽§ Father, Your Son showed the highest kind of love. Make us more like Him.

"He is risen"
That through Him we may recover faith:
in ourselves
in our world
in our God.
"He is risen"
That in Him we may rekindle hope:
for the abandoned
for the despairing
for the dreamless.
"He is risen"
That with Him we may restore love
to those from whom we have kept it
to those who are most near us
to those we will never meet
to all and everything.
"He is risen."

"If then you have been raised with Christ,
seek the things that are above."

[COLOSSIANS 3:1]

WHEN ACTOR ART CARNEY accepted an Oscar for his role in the film "Harry and Tonto," his acceptance speech struck a personal note.

Mr. Carney admitted that he had doubts about taking the part of an elderly retiree. But his agent told him: "Do it. You *are* old."

Although we are told in a thousand ways that youth is beautiful, age too has a beauty that rewards those who are mature enough to appreciate it.

Mrs. Ethel Percy Andrus, who founded the American Association of Retired Persons, once said: "Let's glory in being old . . . We who are older are free to have the conviction, the right, to keep on being in the stream of life. We're challenged to do something to help our communities . . . After all, we *are* old and we mustn't be afraid, but proud of the word 'old.' "

The willingness to embrace reality in a positive way is a key to a fuller, more joyful life. And it can make us a lot easier to live with.

"You will know the truth, and the truth will make you free." [JOHN 8:32]

◄§ Increase our appreciation of ourselves here and now, Lord, so that we may build on what we have.

CREATIVITY REQUIRES A FRESH OUTLOOK—an ability to envision things in a different way.

Dr. Frederic Flach, a psychiatrist, has some suggestions for encouraging creativity:

■ Change your environment, if only your room.

■ Find security. Anxiety blocks creativity.

■ Don't play a role, such as that of the housewife or the pin-striped commuter. You get locked in.

■ Choose associates carefully. People who constantly tear you down can block your creativity.

■ Don't close your mind too fast.

■ Brainstorm. Let your mind wander.

■ Be disciplined. Paradoxically, a certain amount of structure is necessary for creativity.

Creativity is needed, not just for artists, but for anyone seeking solutions. Do some thinking about poverty, hunger or injustice in your community and elsewhere. It may lead you to share ideas where they'll do the most good.

> "Be transformed by the renewal of your mind." [ROMANS 12:12]

> ✥ Help me shake loose from old thinking patterns, Lord, so I may use my mind to make a difference.

WHEN EDDIE LOVETT'S "LIBRARY" burned one winter, the self-educated Alabama sharecropper and his children watched a lifetime colection of 2,800 volumes disappear. Three months later, sympathetic people from California to New York had sent Mr. Lovett 40,000 books to replace his lost library.

His story won nationwide attention when it was found that he had devoted a lifetime to "warring against ignorance" by collecting and reading works of Aristotle, Tolstoy, Plato, Nietzsche and hundreds of the world's other great minds. Books poured in, until Mr. Lovett's 6-room farmhouse housed a library ten times larger than his original one.

"All I had was 43 months of inferior schooling," says Mr. Lovett. "I am warring against my own ignorance, and my battleground is here."

Such energetic pursuit of learning may lead us to self-questioning: How much do we read? What do we read? Do we encourage others to read? Are we conscious of our own ignorance? Are we eager to learn?

> "From your youth up choose instruction, and until you are old you will keep finding wisdom." [SIRACH 6:18]

–§ Make us conscious of how much we don't know, Lord, and lead us to You for enlightenment.

An ATLANTA POLICEMAN may be one of the world's safest drivers.

The Georgia police major has driven over one million miles in city vehicles without an accident during his 28 years on the force.

Major R. E. Nickerson credits his outstanding safety record to defensive driving.

"It's been my philosophy that you have to watch the actions of other motorists," said Major Nickerson. "I always watch out for the other fellow, even though I'm involved in high-speed chases. And I've always treated a city vehicle just like it was my own personal car."

There would be a lot fewer accidents of any kind if we "watched out for the other fellow," to protect ourselves from his mistakes and to assist him in times of need.

We expect others and God to look out for us. It makes sense for us to do the same thing.

"Have the same care for one another."
[1 CORINTHIANS 12:25]

  Make us more alert in our dealings with people, Holy Spirit, and full of love.

Economics doesn't have to be a dull subject, maintains Dr. Norman Ellenberg of California State University. To prove it, Dr. Ellenberg has written a primer in economics now used by about 300 school systems in first to fifth grades.

Far from a dull collection of economic facts, the book gives children lively questions to answer.

"Pretend you are the king or queen of your own country," an exercise on money tells the child. "Without using metal coins or paper money, what would you declare as money? Is your new money easy to carry and store? Is your new money strong? Will it last? Can it be easily divided?"

Dr. Ellenberg says his text "allows kids to see that they already know a lot of economics, but they never knew or called it economics before."

Most of us need to know more about economics. We run the risk of financial disaster if we don't get smart about budgeting, buying, interest rates and all the rest.

"Accept instruction that you may gain wisdom for the future."   [PROVERBS 19:20]

ª Give us greater wisdom, Lord, in dealing with matters that require that rare thing—common sense.

OVER 200 YEARS AGO JONAS HANWAY, an eccentric philanthropist, faced ridicule when it rained. He strode about London carrying an ebony-handled tent-like thing of oiled silk, an umbrella.

And people didn't just laugh. Street urchins threw rocks. Some religious groups even tried to ban it. By not getting wet, they said, the user was interfering with the plan of God. But Mr. Hanway persisted—and stayed dry.

Jonas Hanway died in 1786, but not before seeing his version of the oriental parasol blossom all over town. A street was even named after him.

It's easy to laugh at eccentrics. They tend to ignore many of the conventions the rest of us consider sacrosanct. But cranks and oddballs have written many great chapters in the arts, the sciences—and even religion.

Maybe instead of poking fun at them, we'd be better advised to march to the beat of a different drummer ourselves.

> "Let your light so shine before men, that they may see your good works, and give glory to your Father." [MATTHEW 5:16]

᪐ Jesus, You weren't afraid to be an individual. Take away our fear.

To POLICEMAN JAMES WEISMER, there was "something fishy" about a man he spotted lurking near a Buffalo, New York, seafood store.

It was the man's clothes, the policeman decided. Although it was 3 a.m., the suspect's clothing reeked with the unmistakable smell of fish.

Officer Weismer arrested the pungent prowler and then successfully tracked down his accomplice. The loot, which was recovered, included a bag of clams, two boxes of oysters and 80 pounds of ocean perch that had been stolen from the seafood store.

Evidence of wrongdoing isn't always so blatant. In fact, most of us manage occasionally to cut corners without getting caught.

But God, who reads our inmost hearts, has given us consciences to remind us when we get off the beam. We can ignore them only at our peril.

"Keep your conscience clear."

[1 PETER 3:16]

୶ Holy Spirit, may we be willing to listen to the still, small voice.

HAT DO YOU DO when you have a child who suffers from incurable cystic fibrosis? Mr. and Mrs. Gerald Links of Tallahassee, Florida, took in another youngster with the dread disease.

The Links, whose 9-year-old daughter Bonnie must have constant treatment for the malady, adopted 2-year-old David "not as a chore or a duty but a blessing."

"Because we have gone with a child with the problem from six months to nine years old," explains Mr. Link, "it was much easier for us to adapt to the problems than for a family who didn't know about them. We could not let (David) spend his entire life not knowing the love of his own family, not knowing the meaning of Daddy or Mama or other things we take for granted."

There's no knowing why great trials can call forth great goodness and generosity. But it does happen again and again. Maybe the point is not to seek an answer, but to look into our own lives for ways to turn a "duty" into a "blessing."

> "You will be enriched in every way for great generosity."   [2 CORINTHIANS 9:11]

❧ Father, show us how to be more generous.

ᙁILD GRASSES, DESERT PLANTS, hedges and forest fruits are some of the little-known species of plants that may provide economic and nutritional help for the poor countries, according to the National Research Council.

The Council's report cited unknown species of grains, tubers, root crops, oilseeds, fruits and forage crops with potential for use as food.

"Most of the people in the world today are fed by only about 20 crops," said the report. It urged that world agriculture broaden its base of plant types "to help feed, clothe and house a rapidly increasing world population."

Much of the attention given to hunger a few years ago has disappeared. What hasn't gone away is the fact that many people are still hungry.

Scientists can find new ways to provide food. Citizens —you and I—can contribute to direct relief of hunger and press our leaders to enact policies that help the world's hungry.

"Your abundance at the present time should supply their want." [2 CORINTHIANS 8:14]

ᒼᔑ Never let us forget those in need in our world, Lord, just as we want You never to forget us.

Tiny Margaret Morris of St. Louis, Missouri, thinks her dog Red is the bravest dog in the world.

She may be right. Red, an Irish setter, saved Margaret's life in a dramatic rescue that made front pages in newspapers throughout the United States.

Two-year-old Margaret and Red were sitting in the family car when it burst into flame. Red hurled himself against the car window, broke through it and leapt out. Then he jumped back into the car, grabbed Margaret's collar in his teeth and pulled her to safety.

Who is to say what prompted Red to such heroics? What is gratifying and inspiring about the incident is the further evidence that God has implanted—in man and animals too—the ability to care enough for others to risk inconvenience, injury and even death.

"Love your neighbor as yourself" tells just how much people are capable of.

"You shall love your neighbor as yourself."
[LEVITICUS 19:18]

    Holy Spirit, may we be quick to respond to another's need.

Most OF US WHO SPEND OUR DAYS at a desk know what it's like when the head seems to be filled with cotton. No inspiration. Nothing jells.

Here are some tips from *Executive Digest*. Try them when you're finding it hard to concentrate.

■ Get less comfortable. Stand up or switch to a straight chair.

■ Let in some fresh air and inhale deeply to give yourself a good supply of oxygen.

■ Wash your face with cold water to stimulate circulation.

■ Change your view. Go out for a walk if you can. A change of environment helps to break the chain of monotonous impressions.

At a deeper level, occasional time out can be valuable, too. Think about your work. Is it satisfying? Is it suited to you? Are you involved, however remotely, in providing for needs of body or spirit, in nourishing the larger human family as well as your own?

"There is nothing better than that a man should enjoy his work."

[ECCLESIASTES 3:22]

◄§ Help us, Holy Spirit, to be always open to the refreshment You offer us.

Bᴇᴄᴏᴍɪɴɢ ʙʟɪɴᴅ when he was nine years old didn't stop Lester Loken from helping people for thirty years. In fact, Mr. Loken believes, his blindness was actually an asset.

The 65-year-old man retired after three decades as a counsellor with the Eau Clair, Wisconsin, district office of vocational rehabilitation. During his career, he worked with over 1,000 persons, most of whom had lost their sight.

"I have often said my own blindness was one of my better assets," said Mr. Loken. "It made all the difference in the world. You were talking their language. You knew what their problems were, especially the newly blind."

For every door God closes, He opens another. Look at Lester Loken. He turned personal loss into a way of helping others and leading a rich life. With enough faith and enough courage, we can do the same.

"Trust in the Lord and do good . . . and He will give you the desires of your heart."
[ᴘsᴀʟᴍ 37:3,4]

⌘ Jesus, may we seek joy in serving those in need, as You did.

Dennis Michael Burke is only five, but he's good enough at his dad's job to do it for him.

Burke, Senior, an amateur magician and escape artist, has been teaching Dennis the tricks of his trade. Now the youngster has amazed people in Union Beach, New Jersey, by his mastery of speedy escapes from chains, handcuffs and padlocked trunks.

"It's fun," Dennis says. "People laugh and clap and tell me I'm good. I like it."

"He does keep me on my toes," his father says. "It's a little embarrassing to have a five-year-old son who can do every trick you can do. It's hard to stay ahead of him. I'm going to have to learn something exotic that he won't be able to do until he's older."

Children naturally tend to imitate what they see at home. That puts a lot of weight on fathers and mothers to act in ways that deserve imitation. And to be thankful to God when youngsters surpass their parents.

> "For I seek not what is yours but you; for children ought not to lay up for their parents, but parents for their children."
>
> [2 CORINTHIANS 12:14]

Give mothers and fathers the strength they need, Father of all, to be partners in sharing Your creative love.

CHARLES LINDNER SPECIALIZES in laughter. For 36 years the New Yorker has told jokes, usually mellowed old ones, exclusively to elderly people.

Mr. Lindner, who sells hardware for a living, entertains at centers for the elderly, in nursing homes and homes for the aged. His fee is negligible. He does it because he enjoys it. He got his start as a comic at 18 when a friend took him to visit her grandmother at a nursing home.

The self-styled "geriatric comedian" in 54 years old. He salted a recent program with songs—"If I Were a Rich Man" and "My Wild Irish Rose"—rendered in what someone called carefully, "a cheerful tenor."

"I never get depressed when I see the people," says Charles Lindner, "because I feel I'm helping."

There are people who look at unresolved problems and just get depressed. There are others, like Charles Lindner, who try to help. If you want to keep joy in your life and bring it to others, the choice is obvious.

"Rejoice before the Lord your God in all that you undertake." [DEUTERONOMY 12:18]

⋙ Father, make me an instrument of Your joy.

MODERN "PROGRESSIVE, FREE-FORM" methods lost out to traditional teaching styles in research at England's Lancaster University.

A five-member team led by Dr. Neville Bennett, an education researcher, tested pupils in 871 schools. They found that children in old-fashioned schools:

- were three to four months ahead in reading ability;
- gained four to five months' ability in mathematics;
- ended three to four months ahead in English;
- came out better in creative writing and imaginative use of language.

Dr. Bennett, who admits he began with a bias toward progressive teaching, said that traditionally taught students did better because they worked harder.

Whatever method is used in teaching, the acid test is how hard students work and how much they learn.

Everyone gains when cooperation between home and school help students to get the most out of their class hours.

> "Be attentive, that you may gain insight; for I give you good precepts: do not forsake my teaching." [PROVERBS 4:1,2]

≈§ Lord, help us keep a clear focus on the goals of education.

To the people of Sweden, a red car marked "Läkare" means "the doctor is coming."

Day and night the chauffeur-driven cars, marked "Läkare," the Swedish word for doctor, cruise Sweden's cities answering calls received at the police and fire emergency number.

The house-call system, run by the Swedish Medical Association, draws from a pool of nurses and doctors who may work two or three days a month making these house calls in addition to their regular practice.

A typical night's work for a participating doctor is a dozen or more calls to handle medical problems ranging from sore throats to strokes and heart attacks.

Medical patrol cars are one effective way to bring health care to those who need it. There are others. Until we raise our voices in support of such efforts, adequate medical attention, nationwide and worldwide, will remain more a luxury than a basic right.

"I must speak, that I may find relief. I must open my lips and answer."   [JOB 32:20]

&s   Jesus, You cared for the sick. Your followers can do no less.

Fifty dollars worth of seeds got a nursing home resident out of his wheelchair into a fulltime gardening job in Pueblo, Colorado.

The 84-year-old grower is now raising 1,000 ears of corn and bushels of squash, beans, peas, lettuce and melons on his garden plot.

He used to spend all day in his wheelchair, and he claims that his garden has kept him from spending the rest of his life in there.

"If you want to be healthy," he advises, "just plant a garden."

That's a lot of change for $50: one man kept from being an invalid and fresh vegetables for patients in the nursing home.

How many other worthwhile changes could be brought about with similar "seed money" or even for free? That's a question each of us can ask himself or herself. And the answer may be found by just looking around us.

> "Look to yourselves, that you may not lose what you have worked for, but may win a full reward." [2 JOHN 1:8]

~§ Jesus, make us creative in coming up with fresh answers to age-old questions.

A THEATER OWNER IN MAINE could have saved his business by showing X-rated films, but the "price" was too high for him.

Glen Wheaton owned the Pittsfield Bijou Theater —the only one in town. His business was sinking, but he wouldn't bail it out by a choice he couldn't live with. So he closed the theater.

Local residents and businessmen were impressed by a man who felt a "moral obligation to give family entertainment." The community got together and paid off all financial obligations. Then they formed a non-profit organization to run the theater.

The reopened and renamed Pittsfield Community Theater is a publicly owned enterprise pledged to offer live and filmed family entertainment. Its operator, on salary, is Glen Wheaton.

One person with conviction who makes a difficult choice may light a candle that will bring others into action. That first step by the first person is often the hardest. Are you and I ready to make it?

> "And those who turn many to righteousness (shall be) like the stars for ever and ever."
> [DANIEL 12:3]

&s Help me, Lord, to act on a principle whatever the risk.

THE PROBLEMS FACED BY South American Indians are economic, cultural and personal.

One of the most positive efforts to improve the lives of Quechua Indians in Bolivia is Fotrama, a cooperative started in 1962 by Gerald Ziegengeist, a Maryknoll missioner.

Fotrama has assisted the Quechua to process raw llama and alpaca wool. Spinners make yarn for knitters and weavers who produce sweaters, shawls and other articles for sale in Bolivia, North America and Europe. "We can't keep up with the demand," Father Ziegengeist explained happily.

Fotrama has also trained hundreds of young women in literacy, food preparation, hygiene and moral and cultural values.

Faith in God has motivated missioners to seek effective ways to help neglected people to have faith in themselves. By prayer and action we can nurture our own faith. Who can predict the results?

"Beloved, build yourselves up on your most holy faith." [JUDE 1:20]

᪵ Amid life's uncertainties, Lord, help us to keep our eyes firmly fixed on You.

A FEW AMERICANS don't share the general reluctance to contribute money to the government. Each year, about a dozen send a little help to reduce the national debt, currently $493 billion.

A retired wholesale grocer in North Carolina wrote a check for $1,000. "I'm not a crackpot," said Guy Madison Brook, 73. "I just wanted to do something for my country."

A man in Seattle makes a yearly gift to match his age. The latest was $78. For six years, one man has been sending in checks averaging $75, which he considers his fair share.

"We're very appreciative," says James Spahr, a treasury official, "and we always write a personal note of thanks."

Nobody expects people to send their tax return to Uncle Sam with a smile, or to overpay. But pay we must. And the citizen who pays has the right and duty to make his or her views known on how it is spent.

> "Listen to me; let me also declare my opinion." [JOB 32:10]

  Holy Spirit, help me overcome the inertia that keeps me from exercising my full citizenship.

REUBEN MAURY, a writer, gives tips from his own experience to newly-retired persons:

■ Don't yield to self-pity, slow down too much or neglect your appearance. Walking, swimming and yoga can help keep you trim.

■ Read at least one newspaper daily. Use your library for magazines as well as books.

■ Do you enjoy music? Stereo record and cassette players can be economical and good entertainment.

■ Take advantage of social facilities at your club, lodge, union or church to meet and mingle with others.

■ Enroll in the American Association of Retired Persons (1909 K St., N.W., Washington, D.C. 20006).

■ Finally, help other people. Service is always needed by such groups as the Red Cross, Humane Society, churches, schools and hospitals.

At any stage in life, the active stay healthier in mind and body. Give each day your best, and the years may be a little lighter to carry.

"Bring their lives to fulfillment in health and happiness and mercy."   [TOBIT 8:17]

 formula May we never grow bored with life, Lord, for it is Your gift.

HER SON'S EDUCATION IS COSTING Beulah Hall a lot —waiting morning to evening, five days a week, beside a road with her seeing-eye dog in the hot Florida sun.

Mrs. Hall, a 54-year-old blind woman, promised her dying husband that their son would have an education. But she and the boy live deep in the mangrove swamps of Marco Island, Florida, in a trailer without electricity or plumbing.

Daily, Mrs. Hall and her guide-dog Barney escort 9-year-old Buddy two miles through panther-infested woods to State Road 951. Under a tattered umbrella, they wait all day for Buddy's return.

"I promised him Buddy would get an education," says Beulah Hall, "and I won't break that promise, no matter what it takes."

Dishonesty and corruption in high places may lead you to wonder if anyone's word is reliable. If so, think of Beulah Hall. Millions like her are proof that honor is alive and well in these United States.

"I will fulfill the promise I made."
                                          [JEREMIAH 33:14]

&ed; God, may our deeds match our words.

HEN LONDON GARAGE OWNER Lou Yallop tossed a stale salmon from his freezer into the Thames River, he had no idea what he was to cause.

Later, fished from the screens of a London power station, the 8-lb. 4-oz. adult female salmon was thought to have migrated up the river to spawn—though no salmon have been in the Thames for 141 years. The event was hailed as a near-miraculous result of stringent environmental controls in recent years.

Mr. Yallop recognized pictures of the fish, "because it weighs about the same and it was bruised in exactly the same place. I thought it would be a laugh if some fisherman found it washed up somewhere, but I never expected all this fuss," he said.

There's a tendency in all of us to accept as truth what is more likely to suit our convenience. But there are times to weigh the evidence carefully. It may be less satisfying to evaluate the unfavorable with care. But truth is not a matter of convenience.

> "Pray to the Most High that He may direct your way in truth." [SIRACH 37:15]

❧ Grant us greater objectivity, Holy Spirit, in meeting the daily events of our lives.

YOUNGSTERS FROM NEW YORK'S Brownsville area "wrote their way" into the hearts of towns in New York and Pennsylvania through an essay program sponsored by a local community center.

As part of the Fresh Air Fund program, the children adopted towns, learned about them and wrote essays which were printed in local papers of the towns.

The purpose of the essay program, said Center director Jack Kott, was to lessen the shock the city-bred child might experience from a different way of life, and to remind towns and villages that hosts are needed for Fresh Air Fund children.

"We never run out of kids," said Mr. Knott, "and it's tougher than ever before with the cutbacks in city programs."

We can become so dependent on heavily funded "big" programs that we lose sight of what the individual can achieve. This essay contest is a healthy reminder of what "one-to-one" efforts can do. It deserves imitation.

> "For everyone who asks receives, and he who seeks finds, and to him who knocks it will be opened."   [MATTHEW 7:8]

✍ Father, make us innovative as we search for solutions.

H ANDICAPPED YOUNGSTERS and their families can now go to a "camp without barriers."

Camp Hidden Valley, near Fishkill, New York, plays host to 20 such families a weekend. Disabled children enjoy a camp experience with their parents, brothers and sisters.

"The parents are the bosses in the cabins," says Pamela Galehouse, coordinator of the program. The experience, she says, gives parents "a whole new look on what their kids could do, and parents and children got enjoyment out of each other's accomplishments."

Cabins have toilet and bathing facilities, ramps, wide doorways and macadam paths for wheelchairs.

"We feel very positive about it," says Ms. Galehouse, who found that the family groups fit well together. "They were sensitized to the others' problems."

Too often we have counted out handicapped persons —and their families. Camp Hidden Valley is a reminder of what can happen once we change our thinking.

"Always seek to do good to one another and to all." [1 THESSALONIANS 5:15]

❧ Lord, give us understanding of those with special needs.

NEW YORK CABBIES have joined together in a drive to reach "backseat drunks" through the taxi driver's famed gift for gab.

"It is aimed at alcoholics who enter the cab sober and decide that the time has come to seek help," says one cabbie. "The first day alone we had 25 calls for help—one from a cabbie himself." When the subject comes up—as it often does—drivers tell passengers where they can get help.

Since many New York taxi passengers are from other cities and states, the drivers see the campaign as helping the rest of the country, too.

"Alcoholics Anonymous" speaks about "carrying the message"—the message being that alcoholism can be arrested. If you—or someone you love—has a drinking problem, the message is: Call your local Council on Alcoholism. Help is available.

> "Then let us no more pass judgment on one another, but rather decide never to put a stumbling block or hindrance in the way of a brother."   [ROMANS 14:13]

∾ Lord bless those working in the field of addiction services.

LAW STUDENTS AT STANFORD UNIVERSITY don't learn about prison only from books. They spend weekends as inmates at San Francisco County jail.

"It's to see what life is like on the inside," explains Dr. David Rosenhan, a professor of psychology and law. "We'll learning a lot more, and a lot faster than by reading about jails."

Dr. Rosenhan's students are using the jail as a "campus" through arrangements with the county sheriff, who has sought to open the jail to the community to increase public awareness.

If more of us had first-hand experience of prison life, maybe fewer people would be inclined to break the law. And maybe judges would look for creative alternatives in sentencing. And maybe citizens would insist that these public institutions do more for prisoners than just coop them up.

Like most things in our society, prisons could do a better job, but only if we really want them to.

"Receive instruction in wise dealing, righteousness, justice, and equity."

[PROVERBS 1:3]

≈§ In our search for justice, Father, remind us to be humane and compassionate.

WHAT IS THE MOST IMPORTANT QUALITY of the creative scientist? Brilliant intelligence? No, says Dr. Lawrence Freedman, a University of Chicago psychiatrist. His studies show that childlike curiosity is the most vital element.

"As children, we are constantly trying to find out why things work as they do," says Dr. Freedman. "Those who are able to put existing information together in a novel way to help us understand how and why things happen, never stop asking those fundamental questions."

Only after child-like curiosity and enduring energy does Dr. Freedman rate above-average intelligence as a vital element in the creative process.

Few people ever become research scientists. But there isn't a job—or a life—that couldn't be enriched by mental flexibility and hard work. Look at the world through fresh eyes. Act on your discoveries. Delightful things will start to happen.

> "Call to Me and I will answer you, and will tell you great and hidden things which you have not known." [JEREMIAH 33:3]

   Father, open our minds and strengthen our wills to do Your work.

BILKING SENIOR CITIZENS out of their savings has become a widespread racket, warns the New York City Police Department. It processes over 5,000 complaints involving millions of dollars each year.

"For old people," says Lieutenant Norbert Campbell, "a hope of another $3,000 means another year of life." He said that there are about 26 basic "games" with which confidence men and women work.

Many games are seasonal—offering the elderly victim "bargains" in goods or services which never arrive after payment is made. Some, offering investments in stocks or real estate, cost the unwary retiree a lifetime's savings. The older person is most often victimized, says Lieutenant Campbell, because "that amount they have in the bank is like an index of how long they're going to live."

Caution is a must when any of us is offered "something for nothing." Swindlers will always be with us, so we need to pray for constant wisdom.

"I, wisdom, dwell in prudence."

[PROVERBS 8:12]

❧ Give us a healthy amount of carefulness, Lord, when unusual bargains are presented to us.

NEWLY DISCOVERED FOSSIL BONES now date man's friendship with the dog as early as 14,000 years ago.

Dr. Bruce Howe, a University of Chicago research associate, unearthed the canine bones in a shallow cave in Iraq.

Before the find, the oldest traces of domesticated dogs came from Idaho, and were dated at about one thousand years ago. This means the link between man and dog is much older than that with other animals, such as sheep and goats.

The partnership between humans and dogs is one of many connections we enjoy with the rest of creation. The only abuse that has entered into the relationship of humans and other creatures has been on our part. God's good earth—and all that is in it—speaks eloquently of His care for us. Do our actions speak of our care for the works of His hands?

> "In His hand is the life of every living thing and the breath of all mankind."
>
> [JOB 12:10]

 ∾ Let us praise You, Lord, for all Your benefits to us.

T HIRD-GRADE TEACHER Carol Tracyk of Orange, Connecticut, wears her pupils art work to class, and the kids love it.

Mrs. Tracyk ruled off a two-yard piece of muslin into five-inch squares, gave her pupils marking pens and let each create a picture. The white material soon became a splash of colorful owls, Christmas trees, turkeys, pumpkins and clowns.

The material was made into an A-line dress which she wears to class often, "on popular demand."

"They really never get tired of seeing it," she says. "They just can't stop pointing out their pictures, although one boy was really offended. He said, 'You're sitting right on my picture.'"

We all want recognition for our efforts. When that happens, it seems to make us even more creative.

We can also encourage the God-given talents of others by giving credit and encouragement where they are due.

> "Encourage one another and build one another up, just as you are doing."
> [1 THESSALONIANS 5:11]

✍ Lord, help us use our creativity to make better the lives of those around us.

AN IDLE WORKER AND a silent machine spurred a company president to a small innovation that made a big difference.

When IBM's founder, Thomas J. Watson, Sr., saw a woman sitting idly at her machine, he asked her why. "I have to wait for the setup man," she replied, "to change the tool setting for a new run."

The woman said she felt perfectly capable of doing it herself but "I'm not supposed to." Mr. Watson changed job orders for all workers to include "machine setup."

Production went up. So did morale. Management extended the concept of job maximization, with similar results, throughout the company.

Too often petty or thoughtless regulations put a damper on ability to perform. God has given human beings the creativity to forge harmonious solutions. It's up to us to be aware and to think creatively.

"The fruit discloses the cultivation of a tree; so the expression of a thought discloses the cultivation of a man's mind." [SIRACH 27:6]

May we have enough concern for each other, Lord, to encourage creativity at home and at work.

OR SHEER TOUGHNESS and efficiency, it's hard to think of anything that can beat a tree.

A redwood, for example, has a bark so thick that it resists all but the severest fires. If it is felled, the roots immediately begin to sprout a half-dozen new trees.

Douglas firs that grow on the dry, sunny slopes of a mountain adapt to their environment quite as well as do those which are found on shady, wet slopes.

Some trees have defense mechanisms. If an insect penetrates their barks, an alarm system moves pitch to the affected spot which drowns the intruder and seals off the break like a bandage.

Even felled trees help the forest. The hole opened in the woods admits additional sunlight, which then nourishes tiny seedlings that had been struggling in the shade.

If God has given trees the means of survival, we can be sure He has done as much—and more—for us. Do we believe in His purposes?

"Cast all your anxieties on Him, for He cares about you." [1 PETER 5:7]

   Bring us to a deeper appreciation, God, of Your watchful care over Your children.

HENRY JONES IS A 102-year-old runaway—from a nursing home.

Mr. Jones, who testified before the Moreland Commission about New York State nursing homes, said he ran away at age 87 because "they took all my money and locked up my clothes." Since then, he had "sold goobers and pecans, trying to make a living" until becoming too feeble in 1973.

Still determined to stay out of a nursing home, Mr. Jones asked the Commission only for a little more money to get more to eat, with something left over "to get some pleasure."

Mr. Jones now lives on $228 a month, while it would cost the government $2,000 a month for his care in a nursing home.

Institutions for those who are elderly or ill are needed—but only when people can no longer take care of themselves.

To respect the independence of people is recognition of their God-given dignity.

"Live as servants of God. Honor all men."
[1 PETER 2:16,17]

   Keep us aware of the need that others have, Holy Spirit, to do things on their own.

Gasoline may claim a growing part of your budget, but these fuel-saving tips can help:

■ Keeping a car tuned can give 9-to-15 percent better mileage.

■ Proper tire pressure can add a mile a gallon.

■ Radial tires cost a little more, but deliver 5-to-10 percent more fuel economy.

■ Clean oil and filter cut gas-consuming wear.

■ Slow starts and stops can nearly double mileage in heavy, stop-and-go commuter traffic.

■ Driving at 50 rather than 70 mph can give up to 30 percent gas savings on long trips.

■ Try walking for those short errands. A car started cold and driven for a few blocks uses fuel twice as fast as it would on longer trips.

Walking more and using care in driving can be good for the health and be a start towards the responsible lifestyle that is a must in these days of shortages. Such actions show appreciation to God who put the resources of earth at our disposal.

"The earth He has given to the sons of men."
[PSALMS 115:16]

◈ Remind us to be thankful, Lord, in small ways and large, for the goods of the earth.

Here's a prayer written by Andrew Blackwood, pastor of an Atlanta church, for those who labor after the rest of us call it a day.

"Father, we are grateful for your children who work at night so the rest of us can sleep.

"We are grateful for the policemen who patrol the dark street, who receive our loud criticism when they are wrong, but never a word of thanks as they face constant danger . . .

"We are grateful for the firemen whose life shuttles back and forth between boredom and hazard, never knowing when the bell rings if it's a milk run or the last bell.

"We are grateful for the women at the switchboard and the men who through the dark night pilot the heavy trucks and locomotives and aircraft and buses.

"We are grateful for the clerks shuffling mail at the Post Office and nurses on night duty . . .

"For these and all who toil while others sleep, Father, we give Thee thanks."

> "They keep stable the fabric of the world, and their prayer is in the practice of their trade."   [SIRACH 38:34]

IF YOU WANT TO LIVE A LONG LIFE, check up on your attitude. It makes a difference, says Dr. Leonard Hayflick of Stanford University's medical school.

Dr. Hayflick, a top researcher on growing old, decries what he calls our society's mythology of aging. "It is a form of role playing," he says, "that has in fact made people feel old and lose interest in life."

One mistake our society makes, says Dr. Hayflick, is forced retirement at a certain age. He advocates the second-career approach, perhaps going back to school in middle age to develop an interest one has.

People who retain a zest for life, who are not "put out to pasture," he maintains, are likely to remain alert and active well into their 70's and 80's.

"Society" is blamed for a number of things. But what have we as individuals done for society lately?

Your attitude is your own. You can do something about it. You just might add zest to your life—and the lives of others.

"God richly furnishes us with everything to enjoy." [1 TIMOTHY 6:17]

With your help, Jesus, may we use our lifetime to do Your work in the world.

THE WORLD HUNGER CRISIS is too massive—and too personal—to be left entirely to governments, scientists and other professionals. Here's what one person can do:

■ Samuel Greene, a retired New Jersey man, started a self-help program among the Indians of Guatemala. It is operating now in 17 countries.

■ Dave Gagne quit his job in Minneapolis, simplified his lifestyle and persuaded hundreds of people to join a nationwide fast and send the money saved to feed the hungry.

■ George Cotter, a Maryknoll missioner, developed his own technique for digging over 50 wells in arid Tanzania, benefiting about 10,000 people.

■ Dan West of Indiana persuaded fellow farmers to band together to supply farmers overseas with free heifers to start dairy herds.

Anyone, anywhere, can have an impact. All it takes is interest, time, hard work—and perseverance.

"Lord, when did we see You hungry and feed You, or thirsty and give You drink?"
[MATTHEW 25:37]

✍ Spur me, Holy Spirit, to take a personal interest in my brothers and sisters in need here and overseas.

WINNING RACE HORSE pulls struggling school for autistic children out of money woes. It may sound like a Hollywood script. But it really happened.

Kenneth Mazic, a clinical psychologist, and his wife, Claire, a psychiatric nurse, run Au Clair School in Bear, Delaware. Students range from 7 to 17. It costs about $14,000 a year to educate each child, although some of the 26 students pay as little as $5 a month.

Au Clair used horses as vocational training for older boys. Then, in 1972, with school finances low, the Mazics pooled their annual salaries and bought a trotter named Silk Stockings.

To date, Silk Stockings has earned $351,438. Her winnings have paid the cost of opening a horse-breeding operation to support the school.

It's fortunate that a trotter has put Au Clair School "in the money." But nationally, education needs firmer footing. Only our concern, our cooperation and our taxes can make that possible.

> "To a sensible man education is like a golden ornament." [SIRACH 21:21]

   Make us aware, Lord, of the accomplishments of our schools and ready to help them do better.

NO ONE CAN UNDERSTAND a personal crisis as well as a person who has had the same experience. That was the theory that started North Dakota's statewide volunteer program, FRIENDS.

FRIENDS provides a network of companionship across the state for those moments of personal crisis that come to everyone. Started in 1972 by the Lutheran Social Services of North Dakota, FRIENDS now has nearly 2,000 volunteers and 55 volunteer coordinators.

Files are kept on all volunteers, and each is matched with a "hurting person" who has called or was referred by a private agency, lawyer or hospital.

FRIENDS is now developing a rape crisis center and a child-abuse life-line program. Since it began, the organization has matched volunteers with over 1,750 persons in crises related to death, marital troubles, medical problems and loneliness.

Each of us needs a friend. Each of us can be a friend. With or without an organization, you can take a step today.

> "If you have come to me in friendship to help me, my heart will be knit to you."
> [1 CHRONICLES 12:17]

 Holy Spirit, show us how to love one another more actively.

A YOUNG MAN'S GENIUS in technology may lead the blind a giant step beyond braille.

Raymond Kurzweil, at 27, the head of a Cambridge, Massachusetts, computer firm, has invented a device that scans a page, then reads the contents aloud at nearly 200 clearly enunciated words per minute.

The device, 10 times faster than any comparable invention, uses an electronic camera that sends an image of the printed page to a computer. Letters are turned into sounds and electronic circuits produce speech.

Mr. Kurzweil, who plays classical piano and writes poetry, is married to a psychologist who specializes in reading disabilities. He envisions some day helping her patients with his invention.

We have scarcely begun to tap science's potential for good. While resisting the negative effects of technology, we can help even more if we pray and work to increase its benefits. It's a powerful candle just waiting to be lighted.

"He bestowed knowledge upon them and allotted to them the law of life."

[SIRACH 17:11]

୫ Father, bless men and women working to humanize science.

For Lisa Kaichen, 24, runaway youngsters are both a cause and a career.

A summa cum laude from the University of Detroit, she is director of Sanctuary, a shelter for up to 10 youngsters at a time. She is the youngest head of a runaway shelter in Michigan.

Ms. Kaichen's cause is to redefine running away as an effort to begin to cope with the problems of life, rather than as "deviant delinquent" behavior.

Adults, she observes, have other options. Kids feel locked in. "Many of the things kids are running away from," says Ms. Kaichen, "are things that anyone in his right mind would run from—physical abuse, alcoholism, all kinds of crummy home situations."

"I can't cope" is something a lot of us feel even if we don't say it. We can cope, but often we need help. And we can assist others to do the same.

Whether it's a teenage runaway or a lonely grandparent, there are people who are looking for what only we can offer—ourselves.

> "Be not far from me, for trouble is near and there is none to help." [PSALM 22:11]

  Strengthen us, Jesus, to get ourselves into some constructive involvement with people.

At Chicago's Brookfield Zoo nobody spoils the pumas. They have to stalk their dinner.

Tommy and U-2, the male and female pumas at Brookfield must climb a "stalking branch," which looks like a child's tree house. When they do, a mechanized marmot pops out. If they pounce fast enough, some raw meat appears on a conveyor belt. If not, no food. They must start over.

The idea, say animal specialists, Dr. Gil Boese and Mr. Ron L. Snyder, is to put the "wild" back into the beasts. Zoos, they believe, will increasingly be the breeding ground for endangered wild species. "We have a responsibility," says Dr. Boese, "to the problem of eventually putting wild animals back into the world."

Animals that make no effort get fat and lazy. People aren't so different. Nobody likes struggle and frustrations. But there's a reason for them. Look for it.

"Accept whatever is brought upon you, and in changes that humble you be patient. For gold is tested in the fire." [SIRACH 2:4,5]

ᴥᔋ Keep us ready, Lord, for the crises that will keep popping up in our lives.

ARE YOU A MONKEY, a boxer or a sphinx while you sleep? Dr. Samuel Dunkell, a New York psychiatrist, has classified over a dozen sleeping positions to help his patients see themselves. He believes sleeping positions reveal more than daytime movements.

The "boxer" flexes his arms aggressively, showing hostility. The "monkey" keeps one arm raised protectively, to guard himself. The "sphinx," with head toward the foot of the bed and feet on the pillow, often fights going to sleep.

A full fetal position shows immaturity, says Dr. Dunkell, while a "mummy" wraps sheets protectively around the head and body. The most trusting and giving position, he believes, is on one's back.

Whether or not this theory is valid, we do give ourselves away in many ways. A few minutes a day in reflection may open our eyes to how our daily pattern of action can better serve God, others and ourselves.

"Get wisdom; get insight. Do not forsake her, and she will keep you; love her and she will guard you." [PROVERBS 4:5,6]

⊸§ Grant me insight, Holy Spirit, into the one person whose motives and actions I can correct—myself.

Virginia Beach, Virginia, has made a community recreation park out of 640,000 tons of garbage.

"Mount Trashmore" is a mountain of solid waste that is the heart of a 162-acre recreation center. The park also contains a 1,000-seat amphitheatre and an artificial lake stocked with fish.

Begun in 1966 as a demonstration project under the HEW Solid Waste Disposal Act, Mount Trashmore is honey-combed with 18-inch cells of trash interspersed with 6-inch cells of clean soil. Six feet of clean soil cover the mount's surface.

Constructed in four and a half years, Mount Trashmore has proved to be an ingenious solution for the city's solid waste disposal problems—as well as a new recreational resource.

We have the technology to clean up our planet and to feed and house all of its people. But technology only works if we push the right buttons. Back such efforts with your voice, your vote and your voluntary service. A more human world can start with you.

"Behold, I make all things new."
[REVELATIONS 21:5]

∽§ Jesus, may we care enough to act.

THREE ABANDONED PULLMAN CARS, a baggage car and a red caboose have become one of America's most popular art galleries—the Artrain.

The five cars are equipped with sculpture, 19th and 20th century masters, and contemporary works. A studio car accommodates etchers and lithographers, weavers, painters, potters and jewelers. Three artists travel with the train, and local artists are invited to work in the studio during five-day stops in towns across the land.

Artrain has attracted 700,000 people in its latest 15-state tour. It's goal is to bring art to the people.

What is authentic art but an expression of human life as it touches its heights and depths? In each of us there exists the capacity to sense in our world something of God's beauty. Cherish it.

"I considered these things inwardly and thought upon them in my mind."

[WISDOM 8:17]

 Make us more attentive, Lord, to those things that give added zest and insight to our daily living.

RETARDED CHILDREN AND ADULTS of Sonoma County, California, have some new friends—the Citizens Advocates.

The Advocates—students, businessmen, housewives or retirees—are volunteers who befriend mildly or severely retarded "proteges," often helping them make important life changes and adjustments.

The proteges are in hospitals, private facilities or their own homes.

Advocates often help proteges get special training, or teach youngsters community living skills.

"You don't see too many mentally retarded people picketing for more workshops, for more freedom," says Dennis Pankratz, the project's coordinator. "We work for a group that hasn't been able to speak for itself."

To seek justice for those unable to seek it for themselves is to do a God-like work. Every community has voices too small, too few or too weak to be heard. Will you make their cause your own?

> "Give justice to the weak and the fatherless;
> Maintain the rights of the afflicted and the destitute." [PSALM 82:3]

ê Jesus, like You, may we be a voice for the voiceless.

A SONIC CAMERA has been developed which makes it possible to see through solids.

Developed by Byron B. Brenden of Richland, Washington, the device provides immediate three-dimensional images.

The camera is already being used to inspect weldings such as those in nuclear reactors and ship hulls. Rockets can be inspected for any flaws in the propellants.

Medical research is being conducted for use in the heart field. With such "acoustical holography," doctors will be able to instantly view many body conditions. It will also enable tunnel builders to "see" through solid stone.

If only we had a way to "see through" situations and people, we would be in a better position to be of tactful assistance.

As it is, we can be more perceptive by making the effort to listen—for words and for silences. May God grant us that ability.

"May the Lord grant you discretion and understanding."   [1 CHRONICLES 22:12]

❧ Give us deeper insight, Lord, so that we can be of help when needed.

FTER RAISING 74 CHILDREN, Mr. and Mrs. Jack Lamont of Vancouver, British Columbia, have decided to retire. Of the 74, only two were their own.

Over the past 30 years, the Lamonts have cared for boys brought to them by the Catholic Family and Children's Service. Their top number at one time was 11. Five of the youngsters are now in their 30's and are married with children of their own.

"People used to think we were a Boy Scout troop," Mr. Lamont remembers.

"Oh, sure we had problems," they admit, "but you do with your own family. It usually took about six months for the boys to get adjusted. The community accepted the boys, and that helped."

Seventy-four has to be some kind of record for foster parenthood. It must also take a very special God-given talent—well used. But any of us can make one or two people's burdens our own. It's an ability the Lord has given each of us. And, if we bury that talent, we'll be the big losers.

"Love one another earnestly from the heart."
[1 PETER 1:22]

Jesus, may we see in You a model for loving service.

ADVENTUROUS YOUNGSTERS playing on railroad tracks in New York City may be warned off by a voice that booms down at them from the sky.

If they are, the voice belongs to one of Penn Central's two "Chopper Coppers" whose helicopter patrol clears the tracks of vandals and wandering children.

H.A. Rose and Michael Borachok cruise over the city's miles of rails, dropping their helicopter to about 700 feet whenever they spot trespassers. First a siren blasts. Then a commanding voice says "O.K. kids, get off the tracks." Usually the youngsters stare up in surprise, then back off.

The "spy in the sky" program has definitely minimized accidents for Penn Central, says Lt. Rose.

There are times when we all could use a "spy in the sky" to keep us out of trouble. But God doesn't play hide and seek with us. He trusts us, expects us to be adults. We have conscience to help us decide right from wrong—and to act accordingly.

"Have a clear conscience, desiring to act honorably in all things." [HEBREWS 13:18]

 Keep us mindful, Lord, of our responsibility to live up to the best that is in us.

PLANNING A CONFERENCE? One management magazine recommends these pointers:

■ Assure leadership. If you know enough to call a conference, you must know enough to run it.

■ Keep your group small. Invite known contributors. Keep the problem simple and single.

■ Control, with an iron hand in a silken glove. Keep to the agenda. Keep to the crucial question.

■ Squash squabbles. Listen, then restate in forward-moving terms, if another's language is vague and regressive.

■ Keep the conference brief. You came with one objective. When it's reached, don't sit around lapsing into generalities. A good, single-problem conference, well led, shouldn't take more than an hour.

A well-run life, like a well-run conference, sticks to the goals.

What are your personal goals? Do you become distracted from them? Take a few minutes each day to think and pray about where you're going.

> "He who says he abides in Him ought to walk in the same way in which He walked."
> [1 JOHN 2:6]

Keep us from being fuzzy-minded about where we're going, God, and how we get there.

T HE PEOPLE OF SILVERTON, Texas, believe it pays to advertise—and they have a new doctor to prove it.

When the 1,200-resident town had been without a doctor to staff its new $76,000 clinic for six months, townspeople invested $30 in bumper stickers reading, "We need a doctor: Silverton, Texas."

The campaign got national publicity, and 28-year-old Dr. Stephen Zionts answered the call. He and his wife Juanita have been seeing 20 to 30 patients a day since he began work in the clinic, which serves all of Briscoe County. And the patient load is growing.

"We've already decided we just love it here," said Dr. Zionts. "For somebody my age to move into a $76,000 clinic that has about $20,000 worth of equipment—actually it's just a dream."

Making known our needs isn't a foolproof way of getting them met. But keeping quiet when help is required is the sure road to failure.

Speak up. Keep it short. Do your best. Pray. And be hopeful. Good things do happen.

> "Consider it, take counsel, and speak."
> [JUDGES 19:30]

æ§ Don't let us be silent, Father, in situations where we need a helping hand.

"**L**ADY, I'VE JUST ROBBED A BANK and you're going to have to help me." On her own doorstep, Mrs. Jerry Coffey of Atlanta began a grim adventure.

The young man who had rung her bell, now told Mrs. Coffey to get her child and get in her car. The three drove off—the woman at the wheel, her 2-year-old son next to her and the robber in the back seat pointing a gun at her.

She cried and prayed a lot. At a gas station the gunman told her not to alert the attendant, saying he would shoot him. Finally after three hours, the passenger left them. They were in Chattanooga.

Mrs. Coffey contacted the police, who eventually caught the bank robber who had taken $5,000. She recalled some advice her abductor had given her, "Lady, don't ever open your door to strangers."

Even with the benefit of good advice, it's hard to follow it in an emergency. But the more we try, the better our chances of keeping our heads in a tight situation. Think of that next time a stranger knocks.

"But with those who take advice is wisdom."
[PROVERBS 13:10]

Remind us to be cautious, Holy Spirit, without letting fear dominate our lives.

DRUNKENNESS IS FOR THE BIRDS in Walnut Creek, California. The town has set up a "drunk tank" where spaced-out robins and cedar waxwings can sleep off their hangovers.

The little songsters, on their seasonal migration south, stop in the area to nibble ripe pyracantha berries. The red fruit contains a mild toxin that disorients and confuses the birds, which wander in front of cars and fly into windows.

The occurrence is so common, says Gary Bogue, a local museum curator, that many of the area's animal care facilities have made preparations to treat the birds for minor injuries.

Drunkenness in birds may be unusual. But abuse of alcohol—and alcoholism—in humans isn't. Is your drinking creating problems in your life? If so, remember: alcoholism is a treatable disease. For help, call your local or state council on alcohol. It's in the phone book.

"Be gracious to me; for I am lonely and afflicted. Relieve the troubles of my heart."
[PSALM 25:16-17]

৶ Father, may we use mood changers—including alcohol—responsibly.

PHILADELPHIAN ELIZABETH KOPF, blind and partially paralyzed, is now the possessor of a B.A. from Rutgers University.

A widow with two sons and a grandchild, Mrs. Kopf, 67, plans to write. "I think I have something to say," says the English major, "about avoiding self-pity and never giving up." She was blinded 18 years ago by an explosion in a shop where she worked. Then she had two paralytic seizures. But Mrs. Kopf is determined to be a writer and so far has had several articles published.

"You can start over at any age," says Elizabeth Kopf. "There is always something you can offer the world, no matter how old you are."

It isn't easy to surmount limitations such as age, physical handicaps, or personal tragedy. But there is stimulation in trying to do so.

Take inventory. Determine what you can offer the world. You are part of God's plan—in this place, at this time, just as you are.

> "To each is given the manifestation of the Spirit for the common good."
>
> [1 CORINTHIANS 12:7]

◦§ Lord, help us to recognize Your gifts to us, particularly the gift of Your support.

A YOUNG INDIAN BOY saw the swollen bellies of children in his country and dreamed of some day doing something about hunger.

Now a chemist and nutrition expert, Dr. Sohan Manocha is working in Washington, D.C., on a National Institute of Health grant. His current research is on mental retardation caused by malnutrition.

Dr. Manocha is trying to determine if there is a single period of maximum brain development and just what the span is.

The critical period appears to be before birth and just after. It may be a matter of days, a time when malnutrition even though brief, could produce irreversible damage.

Life is so precious that it's never too early to start defending it and nurturing it. Much depends on our attitude. Life comes from God. How it fares is up to us.

> "For You did form my inward parts, You did knit me together in my mother's womb."
> [PSALM 139:13]

 Guide us in our efforts, Holy Spirit, to enhance respect for human life.

Robert Gainer earned himself a place in the record books by becoming the youngest person to sail solo across the Atlantic Ocean.

Mr. Gainer, 22, made the trip from Wickham, Rhode Island, to Falmouth, England, in 57 days aboard his 22-foot sailboat "Hitchhiker."

Only once was his life in danger, when "Hitchhiker" capsized after falling off a high wave. But the boat righted itself and the young skipper was able to bail it out. "A few hours of being scared out of 57 days—that's not a lot," he says of his adventure.

Over the centuries, the drive to do something that will be remembered has moved people to endure great danger and hardship. It's a drive we all share—at least to a limited extent.

The big question to ask ourselves is: Are my goals worthwhile and what am I willing to do to achieve them? For, as Jesus pointed out, "Where your treasure is there will your heart be also." (Matthew 6:21)

  Father, make us men and women of high purpose.

FOR TWO AND A HALF YEARS, Diane Chechik of Madison, Wisconsin, tried to be a businesswoman, wife, mother and homemaker. Even with her family's support, the effort proved to be too much.

By the time she cleaned house, cooked, did laundry, drove in a car pool, and travelled to Chicago on buying trips for her boutique, she explains, "It was one or two in the morning and I was so hyper I couldn't sleep."

Then she broke out in hives and decided, "Something has to go." So she gave up her business and devoted herself to enjoying her children while they were still young.

Nor does Mrs. Chechik feel any less liberated as a woman. "The real liberated woman," she maintains "is the one who makes choices."

Lack of balance in any life can be devastating. Diane Chechik said she had to "look in the mirror and decide priorities." Is there need in your life to do the same?

> "For everything there is a season, and a time for every matter under heaven."
>
> [ECCLESIASTES 3:1]

~§ Jesus, guide us in the delicate balancing act of portioning out our time and attention.

A DISCIPLE OF CONFUCIUS asked the master: "What are the basic ingredients of good government?" The answer was: "Sufficient food, sufficient weapons, and the confidence of the people."

"But," continued the disciple, "suppose you had to dispense with one of these three things—which would you forego?"

"Weapons," said the master.

The disciple persisted. "Suppose then, that you were forced to choose between one of the two left—which would you then forego?"

And Confucius answered: "Food. From of old, death has been the lot of all men, but a people that no longer trusts its rulers is lost, indeed."

Leaders have to prove themselves worthy of our trust. And we as citizens can help by intelligent and energetic involvement in the political system by which we govern ourselves.

> "Moreover, it is required of stewards that they be found trustworthy."
>
> [1 CORINTHIANS 4:2]

ᴇᏜ Lord, let us never give up our right to vote and make some difference in political life.

ARE YOU SHY? If so, you have a lot of company. For instance, about 40 percent of the college students polled by Professor Philip Zimbardo of Stanford University called themselves shy.

"It is essentially a self-imposed label," said Professor Zimbardo. "If you believe you are shy, you will act it. And it's your awareness of that label that affects how you will deal with people."

Dr. Zimbardo reported that assertive people expressed the same feelings as shy ones in similar situations—nervousness, moist palms, palpitating hearts. Only, they didn't let that hold them back.

Most of us are timid at times. In many cases this trait can be overcome if we get rid of self-imposed labels. If shyness is holding us back, it's worth the effort to overcome it. Each of us has something to offer others that the Lord has put in our keeping.

We won't change the world for the better while hiding in a corner.

"God did not give us a spirit of timidity but a spirit of power and love and self-control."
[2 TIMOTHY 1:7]

~§ Enable us, Jesus, to be better communicators of Your love and truth.

In 1816, a GERMAN FORESTER invented the "Hobby Horse," an ancestor of the bicycle, to use in his daily inspection tours. It would only coast.

A Scotsman, in 1840, added foot pedals. In 1865, the "Velocipede," soon to be known as the "Boneshaker," appeared at the Paris Exposition. It had wooden wheels and iron tires.

Finally, a workable bicycle was shown at the American Centennial Exposition of 1876. A man named Albert A. Pope saw it and had the Weed Sewing Machine Co. of Hartford, Connecticut, make some for him.

In the 90's, cycling clubs and the bicycle-built-for-two were marks of the era.

Bicycling is 100 years old in America. Today its popularity springs from different causes: it is inexpensive, low-energy, non-polluting transportation.

It's refreshing to find a pursuit that has so much going for it in terms of economy, physical fitness and environmental soundness. Consider bicycling. It's a simple pastime with some big payoffs.

"In great or small matters, do not act amiss."
[SIRACH 5:15]

❧ Holy Spirit, guide us as we seek to live less wasteful lives.

GOOD LAW ENFORCEMENT doesn't just happen. It takes active involvement by citizens. Here are some positive things you can do:

■ Be willing to testify if you witness a crime or accident. Don't be afraid to get involved.

■ Help your children develop good attitudes toward police. Set a good example yourself.

■ Let law enforcement organizations know that they have your support and encouragement.

■ Assist in local rehabilitative efforts.

■ Don't invite crime with unlocked doors and windows in your car or home.

■ Encourage efforts to recruit outstanding young people into police work.

Only society—and that means each one of us—can prevent crime.

We can begin in our own family to speak and act honestly. The best law enforcement begins with self-enforcement.

> "For the whole law is fulfilled in one word,
> 'You shall love your neighbor as yourself.'"
> [GALATIANS 5:14]

> ✑ Make us aware that we encourage good behavior, Lord, more by what we do than by what we say.

There is much talk about the effects of TV violence on children. What do the children think?

They've had enough. Too much, if we take as typical the sixth grade of an Alabama school. A social studies teacher asked what the students thought about it. Here are some answers:

"They're always . . . putting all those violent shows on the air," said Barry Creel. "It makes a lot of sense not to even turn the set on."

Some shows, says Kevin Yates, make people believe they can get away with things like cracking safes.

"If that's all you see on TV," said David Blalock, "You'll think it's all right."

Most seemed to agree that there was too much violence on TV and it wasn't fun to watch.

Like these youngsters, most of us feel strongly about what belongs on TV and what doesn't. With effort, we can make quality fare standard on prime-time TV. Watch worthwhile programs. Write to those who produce and sponsor them. Be a force for good in mass media.

> "For you must choose, and not I; therefore declare what you know."   [JOB 34:33]

   Father, bless those working to bring high ideals into mass media.

A HOT LINE FOR TERMINALLY ILL patients and their families is operating in Berkeley, California.

Hoping to "help bury the fearful view of impending death," Charles Garfield, a University of California lecturer, has enlisted 14 volunteers—including psychologists, social workers, students, a priest and a yoga teacher—to answer calls and offer free follow-up consulations.

The 24-hour service is listed under the Hindu word "Shanti" which is near in meaning to the biblical "peace that passeth all understanding."

Mr. Garfield said he hopes the service can remove the stereotype of death as the Grim Reaper and show that death is a stage of existence that can be approached without fear, confusion and denial.

"Mortals" is a word we use for human beings. To be human means to be destined for death. Death—and beyond—is pretty much determined by the way we live, love and face hard challenges. Pray for the strength to live and die in God's love.

> "What you sow does not come to life unless it dies." [1 CORINTHIANS 15:36]

꙳ Jesus, lead us to see each event in life—even death itself—as an occasion for growth.

T 89, STELLA TURNER'S hands are still active. She is a widow in Atlanta, Georgia.

When 60, Mrs. Turner became a practical nurse. "I enjoyed nursing people," she reminisces, "but finally had to give it up when I turned 80."

Then Mrs. Turner started making things. She and some neighbors take orders for ceramic figurines, bowls, pencil holders.

Stella Turner also found she could fix lamps. She makes soap, too, and gives it to friends. Her recipe is in great demand.

"I try to stay busy with my ceramics and doing things for other people," says the elderly lady. "I just don't want to dry up on the stalk."

As we grow older, we may have to resist the tendency to let the world of our interests narrow. And yet, we probably have abilities we've never had time to develop. Finding and using them can make us more the person we were created to be—and brighten the lives of others, too.

"And no one after drinking old wine desires new; for he says, 'The old is good.' "
[LUKE 5:39]

Inspire me, Holy Spirit, to view each new stage of life as "up" not "over the hill."

S PIDER WEBS AND ATOM-POWERED CLOCKS are standard equipment in determining Greenwich Mean Time.

The first astronomer royal of the Royal Greenwich Observatory in England tolerated a deviation of a few minutes in time measurement. But today in the observatory's 301st year, six atomic clocks check on each other for accuracy to one ten-thousandth of a millionth of a second.

The laboratory's alignment telescopes have cross-hairs made of silken spider webs. Engineers prowl country hedges for spiders and coax them to spin webs on criss-crossed frames. Human technology has never matched the perfection of the spider's filaments.

"Marvelous stuff," says an engineer. "Perfectly uniform. Lasts forever . . . and it's free."

The God who watches over the birds of the air and numbers the hairs on our head even provides spider webs for our telescopes. Do we ever say thanks to Him for all things, great and small?

> "Stop and consider the wondrous works of God." [JOB 37:14]

⋙ In our passage through life, Father, attune us to tiny wonders You spread along the way.

SOME PENNSYLVANIA SCHOOLCHILDREN took their responsibilities as "foster parents" to five butterflies very seriously.

After raising the butterflies from caterpillars, the youngsters feared that the cold winter weather would kill them. So, they raised $36 for shipping, and sent the creatures on an airplane trip to Fort Lauderdale.

In Florida, another group of schoolchildren met the plane and unpacked the insects for their winter stay in the Sunshine State.

Butterflies need a warm climate. In any climate, our children need the best care and feeding we can give.

Far more important than the attention we give their bodily wants is how we nurture their minds. And the consequences, for them and for others, are great.

"Bring them up in the discipline and instruction of the Lord."   [EPHESIANS 6:4]

❧ Holy Spirit, keep us mindful that children are people, too.

THE WORLD'S FASTEST RESEARCHER in classical Greek has a metal brain. It does in minutes what once took Greek scholars years to do.

A computer is being programmed as a data bank of classical Greek at the University of California at Irvine. It will eventually store 90 million words to form the first thesaurus of the language.

Traditionally, scholars located and read texts, analyzing word use and recording each word in its context on separate cards.

With the Irvine system, the computer takes only two minutes to find all the uses of a given word in the half-million words of Plato's writings—a task that once took years.

Using the computer will free the scholar for analytical work.

The computer is an extension of the human mind, not a substitute.

Technology is as beneficial or harmful as the human being makes it. Guess where that puts the responsibility?

> "Whoever knows what is right to do and fails to do it, for him it is sin." [JAMES 4:17]

> ✺§ Help us, Holy Spirit, to use modern devices for the advancement of human culture and morality.

YOUNGSTERS AT ATLANTA'S INDIAN CREEK Elementary School learn a second language that few children study—the sign language of the deaf.

In an unusual student exchange program with the Atlanta Area School for the Deaf, Indian Creek's 8-to-10-year-olds attend some classes at AASD, while some of the deaf children go to Indian Creek. Even out of the classroom, students from both schools are getting together on their own.

The program breaks down the isolation that deaf children have traditionally experienced, explains AASD Superintendent Dick Dirst. It also acquaints hearing children with the language and world of the deaf.

One Indian Creek pupil summed up their feelings about the program clearly: "I like these kids. They're fun."

Kids don't usually have the hang-ups and stereotyped thinking that besets their elders. If we can encourage their naturalness, they're more likely to grow into better adults.

"Little children, you are of God."

[1 JOHN 4:4]

    ᶓ Move us, Jesus, to take young children seriously, as You did.

Don't LET YOUR MARRIAGE SAG, says an expert. Renegotiate the contract which, he says, exists consciously or unconsciously in all marriages.

Such a contract, says Dr. Wallace Denton, professor of child development and family life at Purdue University, is "the spoken or unspoken agreement between a man and a woman that governs ways in which each meets the other's needs."

But, he claims, the attitudes, needs and goals of each spouse change through the years. Couples must face these factors together at key times to accommodate change, facilitate adjustment. Some even write down a "contract."

Crucial points could be the birth of the first child, when the children are grown, retirement.

But there's a renewal that could take place every day, in the heart. The words, "I take you . . ." could be updated: "I take you just as you are today." For most of us, that would be saying quite a lot. Try it.

> "Above all hold unfailing your love for one another, since love covers a multitude of sins." [1 PETER 4:8]

 formula Help us, Holy Spirit, to love at the times when it isn't easy to love.

EXECUTIVES WHO HAVE REACHED their limit in a company and face diminished productivity but aren't ready to retire are often unhappy, according to *Industry Week*. The magazine recommends:

■ Keep alert, involved, in touch with change inside and outside the company.

■ Periodically reconsider the goals of your department, the quality of your performance.

■ Establish a close relationship with young people, keep in touch with new attitudes.

■ If you're bored with your job, consider a lateral move. It may provide what has been missing.

Challenge and change keep the adrenalin flowing, the "wheels turning." And the effort to maintain vitality goes beyond the job.

If your job is satisfying, chances are you'll be worth more not only to your company, but to yourself, your family, your community. It's not enough to blame others for job problems. What are *you* doing about them?

"Do your best to present yourself to God as one approved, a workman who has no need to be ashamed." [2 TIMOTHY 2:15]

≈§ Father, You have given me a life to live. May I live it responsibly.

HEN SHE RECEIVED HER SHEEPSKIN from Merritt College in Oakland, California, Bessie Lee Scoggins got a standing ovation.

And a lot of the applause came from the 56-year-old woman's 14 children and 21 grandchildren.

Mrs. Scoggins' teachers called her the star of the child development program. She sums up her approach this way: "When a child has problems, I think it's problem parents—don't down them. They don't need your criticism, they need your love."

Mrs. Scoggins, who is now planning on graduate school, says love of children prodded her into college: "Loving mine like I did, I knew I had more to give and I was going to find those children that need love and don't get it. You've got to get where the problem is and do something."

Getting where the problem is and doing something is a good approach just about everywhere. With God's help, it can propel any life in a positive direction.

"May the Lord make you increase and abound in love to one another and to all men."   [THESSALONIANS 3:12]

  Father, make us willing to strive for excellence in what we do.

PRIDE IN ITS MOUNTAIN HERITAGE transformed Stone County, Arkansas, from a depressed area with 50 percent unemployment to a thriving tourist and educational center.

Nettled by an image of "Ozark Hillbillies," residents formed the Ozark Folk Center as a living extension of the hill people's pride. A complex of 59 native stone and cedar buildings houses craft demonstrations, a craft sales shop, a folk music library, conference facilities, and a tourist lodge.

Over 100,000 visitors enjoy the Ozark Folk Center yearly. And residents have a new pride in preserving their area's heritage.

Self-esteem—in individuals and in communities—doesn't happen by accident. It's built day by day by developing the best that is in us.

If you're feeling left out, perform one constructive act in any area of your life. Do another tomorrow. Soon, you'll start feeling better about yourself.

> "Be not frightened, neither be dismayed; for the Lord your God is with you wherever you go." [JOSHUA 1:9]

Holy Spirit, may we take joy in the fact that we are all God's children.

TWO HUNDRED LETTERS and a market study won 80-year-old Lillian Price's single-handed campaign to change Amtrak's train schedule.

"I did it in a nice way," said the determined Palatka, Florida woman, "but I think they just got tired of hearing from me."

In a two-year struggle to get the Amtrak train to stop in her tiny North Florida town, Mrs. Price bombarded Amtrak officials with letters and a market study of the former railroad center.

Finally, Amtrak decided to allow one train to stop in Palatka each day.

"I just wanted to help make people happy," she said. "We're 75 miles from an airport and we don't even have much bus service."

The voice of the people can be a powerful incentive to action. You and I are part of the people. If we have a reasonable goal, that's good cause for us to sing out for what we think is needed—in a nice, persistent way.

"Do not be afraid, but speak and do not be silent; for I am with you." [ACTS 18:9,10]

ᴇ§ Don't let apathy or fear or anything else deter us, Father, from speaking up for what we believe in.

A TRIP AWAY FROM HOME can be a holiday for you—and for burglars as well. But a few simple steps can foil thieves while you're away.

■ Stop all milk, paper and mail deliveries.

■ Set some lights on automatic timers to go on and off in various rooms while you're absent.

■ Set a radio on a timer with loud volume, to play during the day or night.

■ Turn down the bell tone of your telephone, or place it under a pillow.

■ Arrange to have the yard cared for.

■ Have a friend come in periodically to change positions of drapes and blinds, and change timers.

■ Ask a neighbor to park his car in your drive.

Unfortunately, it's true that we have to take steps to protect ourselves and our property.

But go beyond that. Make yourself aboveboard in what you do. That's a positive step toward an honest world.

"Where there are many hands, lock things up." [SIRACH 42:6]

₰ Keep us from cutting corners, Jesus.

A LONDON COUPLE made a "shift from trivia" because they think the world needs a radical change in values.

Patrick and Shirley Rivers moved to a crumbling cottage on a few derelict acres near the Welsh border. "Our programme," says Mr. Rivers, "is to make this dump productive and beautiful. We feel it is a useful thing to do."

The couple had begun to feel uncomfortable as they became aware of the poverty in the world. Believing over-consumption and want are linked, they shifted to a lifestyle of eating less, buying less, throwing away less and making do with less.

They keep finding new ways to make less count more. And they say they're happier.

Anyone can look hard at the values his or her lifestyle reflects. Try it. If you don't like what you see, consider a change. A shift in attitude can start important things happening.

"To you has been given the secret of the Kingdom of God." [MARK 4:11]

  Father, when I pray "Thy kingdom come," may I understand that I have a part in its coming.

STEPHEN HERMIDES, a 58-year-old Columbia University employee is a "drop-in."

In 14 years, the university library worker has taken hundreds of courses, using his privilege of attending Columbia tuition-free. He has studied Hebrew, Greek, Sanskrit, chemistry, physics, philosophy and the humanities.

"With the Bible as a guide I began matching the courses to the order of creation," Mr. Hermides explains. "Astronomy when God divided the light from darkness . . . Geology when He made the earth. Botany when He brought forth trees and plants. Zoology, with the creation of animals. Anatomy when He made Adam and Eve."

Concluded the perennial student, "A wise and noble mother once advised me that it is beautiful to learn for the sake of learning."

A thirst for learning can do two things: it can expand our knowledge and it can show us how little we know. Both are useful for personal development and for the skills needed to be of some use to others.

> "The wise man also may hear and increase learning, and the man of understanding acquire skill." [PROVERBS 1:5]

ᴥ§ Enlarge our vision of Your world, Father, and give us the strength to be humble seekers of Your truth.

Do you want to get more out of your work day? These tips for executives from *Horizons Magazine* deserve attention:

1. Start with the big projects; save little ones for last.

2. Reserve chunks of quiet time to work on tough problems and on-going projects.

3. Write less; phone more.

4. Shorten or eliminate meetings when possible.

5. Make priority lists to organize your time.

6. Analyze how you spend your time. Record your activities for a month, noting time-wasting activities.

7. Cut out needless reading.

8. Learn to use time spent waiting and commuting.

Busy executives or not, we can all use our time more effectively. If you look at the people who are making a difference, you'll see that they don't waste much time. With a little prayerful reflection, you can put more in your days.

"Conduct yourselves wisely . . . making the most of the time." [COLOSSIANS 4:5]

Father, may we spend more time in Your service.

HEN PAUL VANDERMAAT of Los Alamos, New Mexico, got a speeding ticket, he fought back—with a knowledge of physics.

The alleged speedster, a theoretical physicist at the Los Alamos Scientific Laboratory, was mystified when the police officer stopped him. He had been driving at 25 miles an hour. But he wasted no time in argument; he went home to consult his books.

A few weeks later, the court heard a strange defense. The ticket had been issued, said Mr. VanderMatt, 10 minutes before a thunderstorm, just when the oncoming electricity creates in the air ionized particles that can throw radar out of kilter.

Judge Raymond E. Hunter just nodded and dismissed the case. The judge, who is on the bench part time, is also a physicist at the laboratory.

There is considerable power in knowing you are right, but not enough. In seeking justice, take reasonable steps to act on that knowledge. Equally important, help others to find just solutions.

"Is it not for you to know justice?"
[MICAH 3:1]

e§ Help us, Holy Spirit, to use our knowledge for good.

THE AMERICAN FLAG is the "embodiment in graphic form of the history of our country."

So states Dr. Whitney Smith who directs the Flags Research Center in Winchester, Massachusetts. He has written 11 books on flags of our country and of the world.

The early English settlers, of course, brought over the British flag. Eventually, says Dr. Smith, the Puritans, restless for a separate identity, took off the St. George cross and put a plain white space in the corner of a red field.

Various redesigns preceded and followed the United States flag of 1775 with its 13 stripes. The 13 stars were added in 1778; and by 1816, there emerged the current design with a new star for each new state.

A flag has value only because it stands for the beliefs to which a nation is committed. Our flag stands for America's commitment to the God-given rights of "liberty and justice for all."

Think of that when you fly a flag. Fly it on days the nation celebrates. Fly it on Flag Day.

"Guide the nations upon the earth."

[PSALM 67:4]

∽§ May I remember, Lord, not only my rights as an American, but my responsibilities.

People told Diane Gibby she was too young for college at 16. But the Miami, Florida, coed completed her undergraduate work at 18.

Diane's parents, both doctors, backed her. "I encouraged her," says her mother, "because I understood what she was facing. I graduated from college when I was 19 and faced much of the same opposition back then."

"What people should realize," Diane points out, "is there is no reason to hold a person back because of age. What's important is whether or not I am mature and disciplined enough to do well." Her grades leave no room for doubt on that score.

Diane is now preparing to enter medical school.

Age holds some young people back. More commonly, older people are refused jobs on the basis of age. For young or old, discrimination because of age is illegal. It's also a regrettable loss of desperately needed talent. "Ageism" will never help change the world for the better.

"Aim at righteousness, faith, love, and peace." [2 TIMOTHY 2:22]

Jesus, You took people as they were. May we do the same.

ICTURE YOURSELF WORKING for an airline, charged with checking the destination of luggage. It sounds pretty simple, yet one airline recently spent $5 million to retrieve misplaced baggage. Why?

The task is too simple, claims psychologist Saul Gellerman. He points to an increase in jobs which require a worker to watch for errors or breakdowns in a process where they seldom occur.

This sort of work, he says, is being done by millions. Because they are performing below their own goals and capabilities, such workers often become disinterested. This results in sloppy performance and low productivity —and loss of money.

In a research report, Dr. Gellerman comments: "The right person for any job is one who, with effort, barely can cope with its demands."

Being "on your toes" may not be comfortable. But we are made so that we achieve more that way—on the job, in the family, as a friend, as a citizen. We can help, by expecting the best of each other.

> "Whatever your hands find to do, do it with all your might." [ECCLESIASTES 9:10]

> Ѧ Help me, Father, not to grow lazy and in-
> different in my relationships, particularly
> with You.

Martine Bianchi's visit to New York City was saved by 180 friendly cabbies.

When the 26-year-old Parisian secretary first arrived in town she was charged $52 for a $10 ride by a local taxi driver. Indignant, Ms. Bianchi reported the incident to the press. Soon afterward, she was flooded with telephone calls, among them an invitation from members of the Inter-Boro Two-Way Radio Taxi Association of Queens.

Its members treated the disillusioned vacationer to a tour of the Empire State Building and the U.N., climaxing the day with dinner at Rockefeller Center's famed Rainbow Grill.

Convinced that not all cabbies are alike, Ms. Bianchi told reporters, "I have the enthusiasm again."

Most people are decent, as Ms. Bianchi found out. But no one is perfect. When people or circumstances get you down, try to recall that a loving God has this world totally in His hand. Maybe that will help you "have the enthusiasm again."

"Restore to me the joy of Your salvation,
and uphold me with a willing spirit."
[PSALM 51:12]

✍ Holy Spirit, remind us that it is God's world.

JAMES LEVINE, 28, OF BROOKLYN, is a child-care consultant who practices what he preaches. He cares part-time for his two children while his wife writes children's books.

Mr. Levine has studied 100 men who have similarly broken traditional male/female stereotypes. The study includes case histories of men who have taken on what he describes as "active nurturing roles": a corporation executive, a university professor, an attorney, a public relations executive, a television salesman, several male nurses and teachers.

Mr. Levine characterizes the men breaking this new ground as having high levels of patience, tolerance, independence of mind, security and a strong sense of personal worth.

To nurture the complete child of God that each child is capable of becoming is to build a better world. Whether we have been born male or female, wider awareness of the importance and rewards of this role could, in Mr. Levine's words, "slowly transform society."

> "Train up a child in the way he should go, and when he is old he will not depart from it." [PROVERBS 22:6]

    Help us to realize, Holy Spirit, that the future is in our hands as we guide today's children.

Seventeen graduates, each wearing a long gown and carrying a red rose, walked down an aisle between rows of families and friends. A familiar scene—except this was at the Women's House of Detention on New York's Riker's Island.

Convicted of crimes including grand larceny and homicide, the women had just graduated from a secretarial skills class. Members of the Junior League joined in the applause. They, with city agencies, had sponsored the project—part of STEP (skills training for ex-offenders program).

Some were still serving sentences. Others had completed them or were on parole and had returned for the ceremony. Terry W. gave an address, concluding:

"Teammates, together we have made the first touchdown . . . we must continue to strive to be champions."

Can you help someone to make a new life? Practical assistance is vital, and so is hope. Jesus gave all people a reason for not giving up on anybody.

"Our hope for you is unshaken."
[2 CORINTHIANS 1:7]

❧ Holy Spirit, fill us with more love for people and skill in making love come to life in them.

More and more people are seeking the rugged joys of hiking in the woods.

Hiking clubs are flourishing. The New Jersey chapter of the Adirondack Mountain Club numbered 10 in 1968. Now, 400 members are taking to the trails with maps, backpacks—and zest.

Bob Wendell, sports shop manager in Ardley, New York, marvels at "equipment freaks" who make a mystique of hiking. And he's enjoying the business.

Most are urbanites fleeing smog, congestion and confusion for the clean simplicity of the forests. They are trading their tensions for the relaxation of tramping among the trees.

As the upsurge in hiking helps show, technology, urban growth and progress have thrown us off balance. But we can't just walk away. Each of us has a part to play in humanizing modern life.

Whether you design, plan, manufacture, sell or govern—whatever you do—remember it's your world. If we don't work *for* each other, everybody loses.

> "I try to please all men in everything I do, not seeking my own advantage but that of many." [1 CORINTHIANS 10:33]

> May we remember, Father, that You made us stewards of this world You have made.

IN CHEYENNE, WYOMING, a paper airplane took off and set what may be a world's record—22.4 seconds.

After soaring over a nearby house, the plane floated slowly to earth. Sixth-grader Bobby Miner checked the records in *The Guinness Book of World Records*. The longest recorded flight—an inside one—had been 10.2 seconds.

How did he account for his success? "I used the basic dynamics of flight in the construction of the aircraft," stated the 12-year-old boy. He said his craft had almost been grounded earlier in the day through confiscation by his teacher.

Bobby attributed his knowledge to hours of reading books on flight and many trial runs. He hopes to become a structural or aerodynamics engineer.

Successful scientists often start young, study hard and get support from some older person. If caring about others is the sign of a complete human being, an "early start" may be equally necessary.

"Let us consider how to stir up one another to love and good works." [HEBREWS 10:24]

❧ Don't let us forget, Holy Spirit, that a healthy love of self and others makes us fuller persons.

SURPRISING FINDINGS EMERGED from a survey of nearly 2,000 students sponsored by the Federal Reserve Bank of Philadelphia. Among them:

■ The race of the teacher had little noticeable effect on students' learning abilities.

■ Teachers' scores on the National Teachers' Examinations did not appear to be related to their performance.

■ Experienced teachers produced the most learning growth, except that most low-achievers among elementary students did better with newer teachers who had "undampened enthusiasm."

■ Graduate degrees among educators did not seem to lead to students' learning growth.

■ Pupil achievement on the elementary level was most notable in schools which had about an equal number of black and white students.

In education as in other fields, facts are needed for sound policy decisions. Before acting, get the facts and be honest enough to let them guide what you do.

> "With upright heart He tended them and guided them with skillful hand."
>
> [PSALM 78:72]

&5 Enlighten us, Jesus, so that we may become seekers of truth, unafraid of the facts.

DOCTORS FAILED TO RESTORE the use of his muscles to a 16-year-old brain-damaged boy in Georgia. So his mother has assumed the challenge.

Three years ago, James Freeman fell off a pickup truck onto a country road. He hasn't spoken since. His limbs are twisted and rigid, and he is fed liquids through a tube to his stomach.

When she's around, says his mother, her son laughs. That gives her hope. She intends to try to help him to communicate—and to move.

Doctors who have worked with James say the odds against her success are high. But Mrs. Freeman is taking her son home where she feels he will respond better.

"I'm going to try," she says. "I think I'm going to manage."

Whether or not the rehabilitation succeeds, this mother's love will nourish her son. Try to release the full power of your love in your own family. It might work miracles.

> "Love bears all things, believes all things, hopes all things, endures all things. Love never ends." [1 CORINTHIANS 13:7,8]

ᦒ May Your love, Jesus, complete the love we show to each other.

P RISON CAN GET PRETTY DULL. But a group of inmates in Indiana livened things up by staging their own rock opera.

Ernest Howard, a musician, composed and arranged the score for the musical, "John the Baptist." Father Joseph Viater, a chaplain, wrote the lyrics.

It took Mr. Howard a year to put the rock opera together. One big problem was finding enough men to cast the production. "When you come up with something on the Bible or religion," he said, "you're in trouble for help." But 32 inmates eventually got involved, plus several women volunteers.

"John the Baptist" was presented twice, once before 250 clergy and prison employees, and again for the prison's 700 inmates. It was also played on a local radio station.

A radical transformation could come about in prisons if authorities concentrated on the positive abilities of inmates instead of on their deficiencies. That is God's way with us—and it really works!

> "If a man is overtaken in any trespass . . .
> restore him in a spirit of gentleness."
>
> [GALATIANS 6:1]

    ✑ Remind us continually, Jesus, to aim for the greatness we can achieve.

Ⅰn some areas of Pembroke Pines, Florida, children are illegal.

A recently approved city ordinance imposes a jail term, fine or both, on anyone selling or renting a home in "adult community" areas to families with children aged 14 or under.

One councilman, who was the only dissenting voice, says the ordinance is unconstitutional. Others feel that the move is necessary to protect older residents from noise and "kids running up and down the streets."

City Attorney James Schweikert is sure the new ordinance faces a court challenge. Mr. Schweikert says, "We've already had four or five people saying 'You can't tell me who to sell my house to.'"

Not every problem can be remedied by passing a law. Other ways to resolve conflict include talking it over, bringing in an impartial third party and lining up public opinion.

The next time somebody says: "There oughta be a law," pause. Maybe there "oughta." Maybe not.

> "Blessed is the man who meditates on wisdom and who reasons intelligently."
>
> [SIRACH 14:20]

 ⨾ Give us the wisdom, Holy Spirit, to make the needed distinctions when we're trying to solve problems.

VICTOR PAGLIA MAY HAVE the nation's best bargain in cross-country travel—New York to California for around $60 a passenger.

Mr. Paglia, a 26-year-old Seton Hall graduate, rents Chevrolet vans to groups of eight people for $280 for a one-way, coast-to-coast trip. Passengers share the cost of gas, oil and tolls, and do the driving themselves. It works out to about $60 apiece.

Passengers, usually strangers beforehand, enjoy long conversations, singing, cards and sightseeing. One couple got married after meeting on the van.

Said a British secretary, who took along her 95-pound sheepdog, "It was wonderful—not just because it's cheap, but because it was a smooth, easy ride and a way to meet people."

It often turns out that cheaper and simpler is better. Whether we travel first, second or third class, half the fun is in meeting people. We have something for them—as they do for us. Do we give of ourselves, or hold back?

> "Whether we are at home or away, we make it our aim to please Him."
> [2 CORINTHIANS 5:9]

&ย Make us more conscious of the people around us, Jesus, and their needs.

EXECUTIVE DIGEST HAS PUBLISHED some hints to remember when trying to sell an idea:

1. Discover something the other person wants to do, be or have.

2. Keep your motives honorable. Sincerity and truth pay off.

3. Handle controversial points with care. Start with ideas on which there is most agreement.

4. Remember, people don't like to be told they are wrong.

5. Encourage the other person to do the talking. Hear him or her out. Don't interrupt.

6. Don't force your opinion on others: Make suggestions and let listeners draw their own conclusions. Be ready to concede a point.

The best idea in the world won't do much good unless it is acted upon. Don't let negative attitudes or actions keep your good ideas out of circulation.

Unfortunately, it's sometimes true that we are our own worst enemy.

"Lead me in Your truth and teach me."
[PSALM 25:5]

Father, may we be effective communicators of Your truth.

Greg and Jane Cook turned a graduation gift into an education for underprivileged students.

When Greg graduated from the University of Denver, his parents sent a $3,000 check for a new car. But he and his wife saw another use for the cash.

"Our car is falling apart and we would have liked a new one," Greg said. "But after we spent a semester at Tougaloo College in Mississippi, where many culturally diverse students are helped by the Educational Opportunity Program, we asked that the money be given to EOP."

So the money went to supplement aid for books, living expenses and partial tuition for students at Tougaloo.

The Cooks are among the people of all ages who are turning to a simpler lifestyle and using what they save for efforts in the human interest.

Many of us could cut down somewhere and put the resulting dollars and cents to work in an expression of practical concern. And why not?

> "Let our people learn to apply themselves to good deeds, so as to help cases of urgent need." [TITUS 3:14]

Make us conscious, Holy Spirit, of some good work we could do—and help us do it.

For the citizens of Ann Arbor, Michigan, "Earth Day" led to the founding of one of the city's most popular centers for recreation and education.

When 35,000 people attended a week-long "Environmental Teach-In" at the University of Michigan in 1970, the enthusiasm seemed too good to waste. So, faculty, students and community residents founded the Ecology Center of Ann Arbor.

In six years, the Center has become a gathering place for organic gardeners. Its re-cycling station has processed 5,000 tons of cans, glass and paper. Volunteers maintain a downtown park. And thousands of adults and children attend programs in environmental education, conservation, management and citizen involvement.

People soon lose interest unless their enthusiasm is given encouragement, direction and outlet. Act at the right time, and you increase your chances of success. Now may be the time.

"Behold, now is the acceptable time; behold now is the day of salvation."

[2 CORINTHIANS 6:2]

ᥤ Improve our sense of timing, Jesus, so that we may guide our energies in constructive ways.

Troubled teenagers may be just the "barometer" of a disturbed family, says Dr. John Chiles, head of a family adolescent program at Seattle's University Hospital Department of Psychiatry.

The program views the whole family as the patient, says Dr. Chiles, and may hospitalize one or both parents along with the teenaged "symptom bearer." The average stay is just over two weeks, and parents come to work out their own anxieties.

"Often others in the family system are hurting as much or more than the noisemaker," claims Dr. Chiles. "The family approach allows individual members to examine their roles and interactions. Family therapy reshuffles the cards. It can result in a beneficial new arrangement."

Evidence is growing that, if one person in the family has a problem, everybody has a problem. What is hopeful in this kind of therapy is that one person's shift of attitude can have a good result on the whole family. One person, with God's help, can effect real change.

"None of us lives to himself, and none of us dies to himself." [ROMANS 14:7]

  ❧ Never let us think, Lord, that we can't accomplish good results.

MISS THE GOOD OLD DAYS, before pollution, traffic snarls, crime in the streets, and graft in City Hall? Here are some startling facts from Otto Bettman's book, *The Good Old Days—They Were Terrible!*

■ A century ago, 15,000 horses left enough manure in Rochester, New York, streets to cover an acre to the height of 175 feet.

■ From 1869 to 1890, crime rose 445 percent, while the population grew by only 170 percent.

■ In 1900, 100,000 cocaine addicts roamed our cities.

■ In 1878, members of the New York Police Department were caught cleaning out the Manhattan Savings Institution of $3 million.

Nostalgia, says Dr. Bettman, is "a historical never-never land, misdirected and injurious to our national health."

Looking back and wishful thinking don't change anything.

Even if these were the worst of times—which they aren't—our efforts can make them a bit better.

> "The sand of the sea, the drops of rain, and the days of eternity—who can count them?"
> [SIRACH 1:2]

ᦱᥳ Give us some perspective on the past, Lord, so that we will not feel that the troubles of the present are beyond us.

Jamie Fowler, 4, probably has the world's most widely travelled teddy bear.

Jamie was on a flight from Ngaio, New Zealand, to Kent, England, to see his grandmother, when he lost his stuffed bear. The bear was adopted by Air New Zealand stewardesses, who dubbed it Sir Edward Bear. For three months, Sir Edward globe-hopped from Buenos Aires to Paris to Singapore.

But finally, Sir Edward was recognized by a BOAC crew member, who "bearnapped" it and restored it to its young master in London. By then, Sir Edward was covered with souvenir tags from 150,000 miles of flights.

Most of us don't get to practice thoughtfulness on a global scale like that BOAC employee. But, fortunately, you don't even have to cross the street to show loving concern for another human being. It's something anyone can do, right where we are. So how about making love a bigger part of your life?

"Make love your aim."
[1 CORINTHIANS 14:1]

&ps; Jesus, may we be more loving toward one another.

ᛒEING A GOOD HOUSE GUEST is an art, says Dr. Zigmond Lebensohn, a professor of clinical psychiatry. He lists five important points to assure a continuing welcome when you visit friends and relatives:

■ Leave pets at home or in a kennel.

■ Learn, and abide by, your host's household schedule.

■ Be prompt for meals. Indicate special diets well in advance of your visit.

■ Give your host ample time to prepare before your visit. State clearly when you plan to arrive and how long you plan to stay.

■ Remember that, with relatives as well as friends, brief visits are usually the most pleasant. Don't overstay your welcome.

We probably tend to impose on relatives more than friends. It's a good idea to ask ourselves once in awhile if we are doing to others as if we were the others. It doesn't take a lot of effort to be thoughtful—just a little thought.

> "Judge your neighbor's feelings by your own
> and in every matter be thoughtful."
>
> [SIRACH 31:15]

ᴈ Remind us to take time, Father, to examine our relationships, beginning with our own families.

Do you know what the signers of the Declaration of Independence experienced after July 4, 1776?

Fifty-six men signed the document:

■ Five were captured or imprisoned in the war that followed.

■ Nine died of wounds or hardships.

■ Twelve lost their homes.

■ Seventeen lost everything they owned.

■ Most were driven into hiding.

■ Every one of them was hunted.

■ They were offered immunity, rewards, the return of their property or freedom of their loved ones to desert the cause. None did.

Appreciate the Founding Fathers, but don't regard them as supermen. That would be letting ourselves off too easily.

What they did to achieve political freedom, we can do to preserve it. They knew what they were for and what they were against. God help us to do the same.

> "He who looks into the perfect law, the law of liberty, and perseveres, being no hearer that forgets but a doer that acts, he shall be blessed in his doing."   [JAMES 1:25]

> ⁓§ Make us more aware of our political heritage, Lord, and ready to protect the freedom it contains.

Researchers at Roosevelt University in Chicago conducted tests to determine what would happen if mice were men—businessmen, that is.

The five-year study subjected groups of mice to aspects of the lifestyle of the "typical businessman." The hapless rodents breathed cigarette smoke daily for an hour, had no exercise, ate a high carbohydrate diet, and drank the equivalent of four martinis a day. Result?

The "business mice" lived only two-thirds of their normal life span.

On the positive side, studies on "middle-aged" mice showed the life-lengthening effect of improved diet, larger living space, exercise wheels and, interestingly enough, built-in hiding places where they could be alone.

We human beings have some control over the way we live. Often, we fail to use it. Changing our own lives for the better is vital to any effort to make a difference in the lives of others.

> "My heart is glad, and my soul rejoices . . .
> You did show me the path of life."
> [PSALM 16:9,11]

   Awaken us, Lord, to what we can do to make the world more gentle, more just and more joyful.

TEENAGERS WHO, UH, TALK, you know, like, uh, this, may be victims of, you know, mental fatigue, says Susan Gray, a Los Angeles speech pathologist.

Mrs. Gray, a researcher at Harbor General Hospital, says youngsters may be buying time with the constant interjection of "you know," because television has made their verbal muscles flabby. Another possible cause, she says, is the bombardment of Americans with information, so that "when some people try to express themselves, dozens of thoughts race through their minds—too many for the mental mechanism to sort out and produce the right words."

To parents she advises "Be verbal. If the parents are verbal people, you can assume the child will probably have a good verbal capacity."

One way to reduce such "word ghosts" is to stop and think before we speak. What is it we want to say? A moment's silence is preferable to sounds that signify nothing. In a confused world, it's no small thing to think and speak with clarity.

"If you in a tongue utter speech that is not intelligible, how will anyone know what is said?" [1 CORINTHIANS 14:9]

~§ Grant us the wisdom, Lord, to look at things directly and to think and speak with purpose.

To GO TO SUMMER CAMP in one Miami recreation program, you have to be at least 55 years old. Most of the campers are between 70 and 90.

The four-week sessions keep 40 senior citizens busy learning to swim, dance, make terrariums. They take field trips and enjoy crafts and drama. One camper, 93, is so active that she helps with some of the younger ones.

Arline Miller, the director, says: "It's one of the most challenging and rewarding programs of its kind in the country." She feels that senior citizens of today "are younger and more active in spirit than they were 20 years ago."

Says one enthusiastic camper, "A lot of things I didn't have in my childhood I'm having now. We didn't have time. We were too busy working."

An attitude of "why not?" gets far more done than all the "I can'ts" in the world. Ask God's aid in seeking to become the fullest "you" that you can be.

"Ask in faith, with no doubting."
[JAMES 1:6]

ఆౖ Open our eyes, Holy Spirit, to the possibilities all around us.

WHEN MENTAL HEALTH WORKERS and police teamed up to fight crime in Erie, Pennsylvania, everyone was surprised by the results.

"The social service people thought the police were dumb cops," said Police Chief Sam Gemelli, "and the police thought the psychiatrists were bleeding heart do-gooders. Now the shrinks are like part of the department; we're like one big happy family."

The two departments formed a 24-hour "Family Intervention Crisis Unit" because "the police were making no dent in crime and the county mental health program was making no dent in mental health care."

In many cases, our world has become so specialized that one group of experts has no idea what another group is doing. The result can be duplication, conflict and wasted effort.

Whatever our field, we can learn much from others—provided we admit our limitations and remain open to the ideas of those around us.

"Then you will understand righteousness and justice and equity."   [PROVERBS 2:9]

 ☙ Bring more people together, Lord, to work for worthwhile goals.

A FRIEND OF THE CHRISTOPHERS in Kansas City, Kansas, who describes herself as "a busy 56-year-old homemaker" writes that these are four things she tries to do each day:

1. Do something you *don't* want to do.

2. Do something you *do* want to do.

3. Be quiet a few minutes for special prayer, spiritual reading or meditation.

4. Reach out in *some* way *every single* day to someone else.

"You know," she claims, "it really works!"

The Christophers tell people, "You can make a difference. You can light a candle." That friend in the midwest has set out a simple but effective formula by which anyone can start.

Every life has opportunities for getting out of self, reaching out to others and maintaining contact with God. So does yours. If you look, you won't be disappointed. "It really works!"

"He who is faithful in very little is faithful also in much." [LUKE 16:10]

❧ Father, lead us to You through the small events of each day.

Locking your car helps prevent car theft, but there is lots more you can do.

■ Avoid parking your car in unlighted, unattended parking lots, especially in busy metropolitan areas.

■ Don't leave your car at the airport if you're taking a trip by plane. Tires, accessories or the car itself could be gone when you return from a plane trip.

■ If you commute to work by train, park your car where's it's not isolated. A lot can happen in eight hours.

■ If possible, garage your car every night.

■ Finally, carry good theft coverage in your auto insurance policy.

It's a melancholy thought that our possessions are fair game for anybody with the desire and the skill to separate us from them.

So precautions must be taken. Attention must be paid. But, beyond a certain point, concern about the things we own robs us of the joy of using them.

Life is more than the sum total of our possessions. It has more to do with what we are than what we have.

> "Lay up for yourselves treasures in heaven, where neither moth nor rust consumes and where thieves do not break in and steal."
>
> [MATTHEW 6:20]

> ✌ Keep us from being owned, Jesus, by the things we possess and help us to be generous in giving.

Mary Rigney got an idea of what dying is like. The experience taught her how to live.

At 36, the California woman reacted violently to medication for a minor infection. She had the equivalent of second-degree burns all over her body and was given a 50-50 chance to live.

In what she thought were her last minutes, she had a "feeling of getting ready to go somewhere, a feeling of expectation," then became unconscious.

But she lived. "I know what's important in life," says Mrs. Rigney. "The other things—striving to get ahead . . . worrying about what other people think of you—these things don't matter." What matters? "Being here to see my daffodils grow . . . watching my kids walk off to school . . ."

When we get down to basics, who we are means a lot more than how much we've got. And those we love become more precious.

What's important in your life? What are you doing about it?

> "For what does it profit a man if he gains the whole world and loses or forfeits himself?" [LUKE 9:25]

❧ Deepen our sense of values, Lord, while there is time.

THE DOGS IN A HOMESTEAD, FLORIDA, obedience class had nothing on Porky, the Precocious Pig. The 12-week-old porker turned out to be the biggest ham in the class, learning in record time how to bow, walk on a leash and beg for a cookie.

Jeanne Reynolds, 12, and her brother Kenny, 11, decided to enroll their pet pig in a canine obedience class after their veterinarian told them pigs were smarter than dogs. The instructor, Jean Cole, found Porky bright, but unlike canines.

"Pigs couldn't care less about praise," she says. "You've got to feed them to get them to learn. Maybe that shows they're smarter." She said that Porky quickly learned to heel and walk on a leash. As for rewards, he happily accepted dog food, avocados, French fries, "or just about anything else he can swallow."

Who would think a pig could do tricks? But maybe it bears out the old saw—"How will you know if you don't try"? Have you stretched your mind lately?

"The plans of the mind belong to man."
[PROVERBS 16:1]

୫ Father, may we be open to the wonders of the world around us.

IN WASHINGTON STATE, PRISONERS work with Head-start children and make a new start themselves.

When Vincent Lombard, a state penitentiary super-intendent, married the director of the local Headstart program, they enlisted inmates of the minimum secu-rity section to help with the pre-schoolers. Each day, three men teach arts and crafts, ethnic culture and speech therapy. Others repair toys in the prison shops and cook hot lunches.

"There's a pool of talent you wouldn't believe up there on the hill," says Mrs. Lombard, who estimates that the building skills of inmate volunteers have saved the program $5,000. An added value, say the Lombards, is the program's help in preparing prisoners to return to society.

Rehabilitation appears to work only when prison personnel and others are sincerely concerned about what happens to inmates. As elsewhere in our society, things start to happen only when people care.

"So then, as we have opportunity, let us do good to all men."　　　[GALATIANS 6:10]

વ§　Make us more conscious of other people, Lord, in a real and not a superficial way.

Psychiatrist Louis F. Rittelmeyer of Georgetown University, Washington, D.C., offers hints for growing old gracefully:

■ Accept yourself as you are, not as an age bracket, and take others as they are.

■ Keep occupied, defining what is useful and enjoyable for *you*.

■ Don't try to cling to youth, to your children or try to correct your parental mistakes with your grandchildren.

■ Live where you know people and enjoy activities.

■ Enjoy hobbies, leisure, a part-time job.

"You'll feel young at 80," says Dr. Rittelmeyer, "if you see yourself as an appealing, productive person with contributions to make and wake up with zest for each day ahead."

Age is like the weather. We can't realistically do much but accept it. So do yourself a favor. Stop looking for gray hairs and look for ways to make a difference. You'll be glad you did.

"Choose life."   [DEUTERONOMY 30:19]

✌ Holy Spirit, teach us to live each moment fully.

ALGAE MAY BE THE ULTIMATE FOOD and fuel source for a hungry and power-starved world, says biologist Victor Kollman of Los Angeles Scientific Laboratory.

Dr. Kollman says one acre of land anywhere could produce annually 1,460 tons of high protein algae which could be used for food, and to make large amounts of hydrogen for fuel and of methane gas for fertilizer. The farmer could earn a $1.5 million profit.

"I know the figures sound unbelievable," says Dr. Kollman, "but then, what has been accomplished by man's understanding and manipulation of natural processes has always staggered the imagination."

Dr. Kollman and his colleagues used lasers to step up photosynthesis and production of algae.

The purpose of science is to serve humanity. No one discovery or process will solve the world food shortage. But each is part of a widespread effort to do something so that "all may eat." And each of us can help.

> "The vision that he sees is for many days hence, and he prophesies of times far off."
> [EZEKIEL 12:27]

⋖§ Give us the vision to see hunger in terms of people we can help, Lord, not statistics that overwhelm.

POLICE OFFICERS STAFFING communications units in Suffolk County, New York, will soon be freed for active duty by 70 physically handicapped persons.

In a two-year experiment, the handicapped workers will play a major role in filling desk jobs that are now keeping trained police officers from vital law enforcement roles. Senator Leon Giuffreda, who sponsored the bill for the program in the New York State Senate, feels the measure will help people who are often denied work. Said the senator:

"Pilot programs such as these enable the handicapped to demonstate that they have the ability to work and become more a part of the mainstream of society."

There are many tasks handicapped persons can do, if only others let them—and encourage them. In your office or neighborhood, are there jobs that could be fitted to the talents of the handicapped? If so, you will do yourself—and them—a favor by taking the first step toward hiring the handicapped.

"Whatever you do, do all to the glory of God." [1 CORINTHIANS 10:31]

Let us look more to what other persons can do, Jesus, and less at what they cannot.

Twenty million Americans lie awake at night, says Dr. William Dement of Stanford University. To research insomnia, the school has set up a specially equipped dormitory, "Insomnia Hotel."

"There might well be 100 entirely different causes of troubled sleep," says Dr. Dement, "but until we have the opportunity to study hundreds of sufferers, we just don't know."

Past studies have found two causes—noctural myoclonus, a twitching of the leg muscles during sleep, and apnea insomnia, in which the sleeper stops breathing and awakens.

Dr. Dement hopes to identify these and other causes through observation and brain wave analysis of insomniac and normal volunteers.

The scientific method examines carefully all possible causes before coming to any conclusions. In our lives, fewer bad judgments would be made if we did the same. Wisdom is God's gift, but it calls for human cooperation.

"The wisdom from above is first pure, then peaceable . . . without uncertainty or insincerity." [JAMES 3:17]

✎ Move us, Holy Spirit, to be more responsive to Your signals in our lives.

FIFTY-FOUR ELDERLY handicapped people were within two weeks of losing their social center when a man walked in and offered $150,000 to keep it open.

The man was heavyweight champion, Muhammed Ali. The night before he had seen a televised story of the plight of the Hillside Aged Program Center in New York. It had run out of funds and the handicapped old people were unable to get to other centers.

Mr. Ali arrived unannounced at 9:30 a.m. "I understand you need a lot of money to stay open . . ." he said. "I'll give it to you."

As news of the rescue reached the elderly men and women, they crowded around the donor, greeting him with tears and thanks.

"Service to others," he said, minimizing the gift, "is the rent I pay for my room here on earth."

Each of us takes up some room on this earth—and what we do for ourselves and for other people can be considered a form of rent. To hold back isn't fair to ourselves or to them. Paid your rent lately?

> "As each has received a gift, employ it for one another, as good stewards of God's varied grace." [1 PETER 4:10]

    Make us more aware of what we are, Holy Spirit, and what we can be.

Some of Niki Summers' friends had muscular dystrophy, and she wanted to raise money to fight it—maybe $10. She planned a neighborhood carnival. Niki was 11.

She held her carnival on a sunny summer day in Seattle's Magnolia district. There was a fish pond, penny-drop and ring-toss. Lemonade stands did a land-office business. The house plant booth sold out.

Niki planned it all. Her friends staffed booths and games. One of her sisters was a clown, another a magician. Her mother did the bookkeeping. A man who wished to be anonymous appeared with a cotton candy machine.

Receipts were $106.93. "I want to make a million dollars," said the exuberant Niki. "I really want to help those kids who can't run and play like I can."

Do you know someone with a need you could meet? Even part way? If you start, maybe others will join you. What Niki Summers did, you can do too.

"Go and do likewise."   [LUKE 10:37]

   ᴈ§ Don't let us be scared by the size of the job to be done, Lord, but encouraged to begin.

DID YOU EVER, AS A CHILD, collect fireflies in glass jars on summer nights? Today "the firefly system" is shedding light on heart disease and muscular dystrophy.

The "system" involves using the insect's light-producing chemicals to test for the presence of ATP, an energy storage compound contained in all living cells. The amount of light generated is in direct proportion to the ATP present.

This, in turn, indicates the presence of another chemical which usually accompanies cardiac arrest or muscular dystrophy. The "firefly system" can be used as an immediate test for heart attack. It is also a quick way to find muscular dystrophy, especially in newborn infants.

To these medical uses, we can still add enjoyment of the glow of fireflies on a summer's evening. Perhaps they will deepen our awareness of the Creator who made so many things good, true and beautiful.

"Make all men see what is the plan of the mystery hidden for ages in God who created all things." [EPHESIANS 3:9]

৺ Let us lift up our eyes, Father, to the wonders of Your world—and ours.

WALLY DURBIN'S WIFE DOESN'T CARE if her husband gets into "monkey business." That's how he supports the family.

Mr. Durbin, of Toledo, Ohio, decided to sell his service station and go into partnership with a monkey. For three years he has travelled from Florida to California, grinding away at a hand organ while his monkey, Freddie, collects coins. On good days, he makes as much as $80.

"A lot of my friends thought I was nuts," says Mr. Durbin, who believes he is one of only eight organ-grinders with monkeys in the U.S. But his wife sees no problem. Says she:

"It's what he wants to do and as long as he makes enough to support us, it's fine with me."

Sometimes we have to face the opposition of friends to do what we think is right. We generally do better if we act on our conclusions, not their expectations.

To become our best selves is the best gift we can make to family, friends and God.

> "You, therefore, must be perfect as your heavenly Father is perfect."
>
> [MATTHEW 5:48]

᪥ Bring us to be more self-directed, Lord, less dependent on the opinions of others.

To many motorists in Nairobi, Kenya, they are a nuisance or a threat. They roam the streets of the city in packs, sleeping in the streets, in caves or under bushes. Ranging in age from 5 to 15, they are known as the Parking Boys.

Parking Boys try to make a few shillings by finding a space for cars in this crowded city. Until recently, little was done for them. The police would sometimes jail them for vagrancy.

Then Arnold Grol of the White Fathers saw them for what they really are—human beings who need help. Father Grol gradually won their confidence, got help from the YMCA and the Red Cross and began filling some of their urgent medical needs.

The majority of the boys asked, not for food or clothes, but for an education. Space was found at the Catholic chaplaincy of Nairobi University and volunteers are now teaching them to read and write.

Here, as in Africa, nothing happens till someone cares. Do you and I care? How much?

> "If you have come to me in friendship to help me, my heart will be knit to you."
> [1 CHRONICLES 12:17]

 ✑ Open our eyes, Jesus, to see people, not as strangers, but as potential friends.

MANY PEOPLE STAY BROKE, says Dr. Kent Baker, an authority on personal finances, simply because they don't know how to manage their money.

Here's the wrong way:

1. Fail to plan or to set objectives.
2. Do not set up an emergency fund.
3. Fail to comparison shop when buying anything from food to insurance.
4. Buy on impulse and end up with more than you need.
5. Try to keep up with the Joneses.
6. Overuse credit.
7. Do not take advantage of consumer information.
8. Do not wait to buy items on sale.

Turn that list around, and you've got a good start toward financial stability, if not security.

The lust for money has caused many individuals and institutions to do much damage. But irresponsible spending has probably done at least as much harm.

"Keep your life free from love of money."
[HEBREWS 13:5]

  Give us greater realism, Lord, in the way we think of and use all Your resources.

THERE IS MORE AND MORE GREEN in homes across the land. People are branching out from ivy and begonias to more and more esoteric varieties of house plants. Courses in plant-growing flourish. Why?

Dr. Norbett L. Mintz, associate psychologist at McLean Hospital in Boston, has suggested a few reasons: the need of our crowded population to keep in touch with its rural heritage; the reassurance of nature's order and beauty in a chaotic world.

Also, says Dr. Mintz, growing plants may help satisfy our basic need for commitment. He quotes Antoine de Saint Exupery's "The Little Prince": ". . . But in herself alone she is more important than all the hundreds of other roses: because it is she that I have watered . . . You become responsible for your rose . . ."

Service brings us closer to the served, establishes a relationship needed by both. Opportunities for commitment exist in everyone's life. Plants may need loving care. But so do people.

"Through love be servants of one another."
[GALATIANS 5:13]

Lord, help us to commit ourselves even in small ways to caring for others.

WHEN THE PRESIDENT OF A major manufacturing company was faced with a feud between executives of his research and production staffs, he sent representatives of both on a week-long raft trip.

Forced to act as a team on the river, the group quickly ended the dispute. Colorado's Outward Bound operates the raft trips which are taken by many executives, including corporate presidents.

"We eliminate the phoniness of the chain of command," says O.B. president Joseph Nold, "and allow them to share a raw experience with their peers." On the other hand, midway in the trip each participant is sent into the woods alone for a 24-hour survival and reflection period.

One company uses the courses in hiring "unemployables." If they make it, they get the job.

The pressure to compete comes early. It can be good. But it can also be destructive. Cooperation with our family and co-workers is at least equally important. Remember, no one can make it alone.

"Let there be no strife between you and me." [GENESIS 13:8]

    Keep us alert to the fact that we were created to live and work in harmony with other people, Lord.

T WO SEATTLE THIEVES have a new respect for "disabled" Basil Stubblefield.

The would-be robbers decided they had the easiest of jobs when Mr. Stubblefield, 29, dropped his wallet on the ground. He walks with a cane and has metal braces on his legs.

As the thugs dove for the wallet, Mr. Stubblefield struck one with his cane and kicked the other with his metal-braced leg. The thieves fled.

Mr. Stubblefield, a victim of muscular dystrophy, had been a karate expert before he was stricken.

If good always triumphed, there probably wouldn't be much merit in leading a moral life.

But each of us can do something to assure that the world around us enjoys a little more justice, a little more peace and a little more caring.

We don't live in the best of all possible worlds. We can, however, narrow the distance between the way things are and the way they could be.

> "Blessed are those who hunger and thirst for righteousness, for they shall be satisfied."
> [MATTHEW 5:6]

ᒬᔒ Deepen our sense of responsibility, Jesus, to ourselves and to those who depend on us.

EVERY DAY, THE AVERAGE AMERICAN is exposed to about 250 TV commercials and radio, newspaper and magazine ads. In a year, almost 100,000 ads batter his senses, but only a small percentage are effective, says ad expert Ed Papazian.

Mr. Papazian, a former agency vice-president, says that people have built up "boredom barriers" as defenses against the flood of advertising.

"The public's been so bombarded with TV commercials and ads," he says, "in most cases, the entertainment value of the commercial—such as the music—passes through the boredom barrier, but the basic sales claim doesn't."

At present, advertising foots most of the bill for TV, radio and print media.

Your support of good ads—by buying the product and letting the maker know you appreciate tasteful, constructive ads—can be a force for good in the mass media. And it will spare your eyes and ears a little, too.

"Approve what is excellent."
[PHILIPPIANS 1:10]

  Father, may we be concerned consumers.

TEN YEARS AFTER THE FACT, an anonymous caller in Detroit apologized over the phone for an act of vandalism he committed when he was 13.

Dorothy Wolfe and her husband Irving recalled the time "some kid" had thrown paint remover and tar on their car and garage. The vandal was grown now, with a wife, child and a home of his own.

That wasn't all. Right after the call, during which the cost of repair, $100, had been discussed, the Wolfes found the first of several envelopes, placed in their mail box, each containing $15.

"It must be a one in a million thing," said Irving Wolfe, "where a man's conscience will take him that far."

Conscience is a strange thing. It can keep us awake or give us a peaceful night's sleep. It can gnaw at us. Or it can turn our lives around from guilt-ridden discomfort to the serenity of a peaceful heart. Do you heed your conscience? It will take you as far as you let it.

"Appeal to God for a clear conscience."
[1 PETER 3:21]

ख़§ Father, may we heed the proddings of conscience.

ANG LO PENG IS A YOUNG FARMER in Taiwan. He fell in love with a young woman in the next town.

So enamoured was he that he wrote her love letters every day for nearly two years—more than 700 in all.

The result? She married the postman.

All things considered, the ardent swain may have been better off that his protestations of love were not accepted. But it would have been hard for him to appreciate that verdict in the first flush of disappointment.

How many times in our lives have we been able to look back on what appeared to be defeats, only to recognize by hindsight that they were well-disguised blessings?

Nobody likes to be turned down. But if life teaches us anything, it might be that God's plans are different from ours. And better.

> "I know the plans I have for you, says the Lord, plans for welfare and not for evil, to give you a future and a hope."
>
> [JEREMIAH 29:11]

ِ Strengthen us, Father, to accept letdowns gracefully and to learn from them.

A "SUN FARM," WHERE SOLAR ENERGY is harvested, converted chemically and stored is the dream of inventor Talbot A. Chubb of Arlington, Virginia.

The solar physicist, working at the Naval Research Laboratory, has devised a system, called Solchem, which collects concentrated sunlight, mixes it in a reaction chamber with sulphur trioxide, and stores the heat in an underground salt pool.

Dr. Chubb foresees a time when "sun farms" in the south and west could harvest solar heat sufficient to run whole cities. His major problem now is building collectors— the 60-foot scoops which gather the sunlight— cheaply. Each scoop now costs almost a million dollars, but would have to cost only $20,000 to make sun farms economically feasible.

So often, important discoveries are made by men and women working alone, or with a small group. The creative process seems to flourish in "smallness." So don't let the thought that you're only "one person" stop you.

"Excel in all that you do." [SIRACH 33:22]

ಆೃ Stir me, Holy Spirit, to appreciate more fully that I am somebody and can do something.

T HAT MAJOR KILLER, STRESS, can be relieved by four basic principles of transcendental meditation, says Dr. Herbert Benson. Dr. Benson lists these four "secret weapons against stress":

1. Quiet;
2. A metal device (a simple, neutral word or sound to repeat, like the word "one");
3. A passive attitude;
4. A comfortable position.

Dr. Benson writes that tests have shown that those who learn and practice relaxation enjoy lowered blood pressure and a slowing of all distressed systems. They also gain lowered anxiety and an increased sense of well-being.

Try this: If you know you're late for an appointment and can't do anything about it, stop looking at your watch.

Constantly reminding yourself how late you are won't get you there any earlier. It'll just increase your stress level.

"Cast your burden on the Lord and He will sustain you." [PSALM 55:22]

❧ Make us more aware of Your presence, Lord, so that we can rest in You.

JUBAL HALE MAY BE UNIQUE in the history of the U.S. Civil Service. He recently asked Congress to abolish his job.

Mr. Hale is the $19,693-a-year secretary of the Federal Metal and Nonmetallic Mine Safety Board of review. The board was set up in 1971 to hear appeals involving mines other than coal mines. It has cost taxpayers $200,000. But it has no work.

Mr. Hale said he spends most of his time drinking coffee and listening to Beethoven records. He told a Senate committee, "I don't think you have any choice but to abolish the board." The Senator chairing the hearing promised prompt action.

Obscure committees, boards and bureaus are tucked away in many federal, state, and city agencies. But it's refreshing to find someone with a job at stake who is willing to talk about it.

People of principle—inside the system—can help keep democracy working—and honest. They deserve our prayers and support.

> "The utterance of a sensible man will be sought in the assembly, and they will ponder his words in their minds."   [SIRACH 21:17]

    Father, bless dedicated civil servants.

A TRIP TO THE COUNTRY can be just as important for old people as for young, says Virginia Taylor of Warner, New Hampshire.

Ms. Taylor, a professional photographer, has joined geriatrics specialist Martha Nobel in a non-profit corporation to turn her small tree farm into a recreation area for the elderly.

"Everybody talks about getting kids out of the city to see what a cow looks like. Some old people have never seen a cow either," says Dorothy Richmond, one of the organization's board members.

Dozens of elderly came for the dedication picnic, wandering among the trees, looking at the stream and listening to the birds. Said Ms. Taylor:

"It's just a place where you can come down and take a walk, and wade in the river in the summer."

Being thoughtful of older people is a good way to grow. Putting ourselves in the other persons shoes helps us to fill our own more adequately. Now is a good time to start.

"And above all these put on love, which binds everything together in perfect harmony."   [COLOSSIANS 3:14]

❧ Increase our sensitivity to other people, Father, as You are Lord of all.

ONE OF MANKIND'S STRONGEST URGES, says the Royal Bank of Canada's monthly newsletter, is the desire to do something to make things better. The letter lists some guidelines toward achieving that goal:

■ Think big. A superior person comprehends not only his own job but those that contribute to it.

■ Look for a vacuum and expand into it. Seek out the machine not yet invented, the social ills not yet cured. Chance and luck don't count.

■ Work with people. Like them, learn from them.

■ Spell out your purpose. Whatever you want to do, understand your purpose and plan your method.

■ Keep on learning. You will never have "all the facts," but you can learn how to find them.

■ Be patient, hopeful and expectant. Believe in what you are doing, and persevere.

If we try to do better, chances are we'll get further than we expect. We have our limits, but we also have our abilities. God wants us to use those talents, and others have a right to the best we can give.

> "We exhorted each one of you and encouraged you and charged you to lead a life worthy of God."　　[1 THESSALONIANS 2:11,12]

ᴇᴋ You never let us down, Lord, and with that kind of help, we need never be discouraged for long.

A THUNDERBOLT STRUCK teenager Greg Lehrer in the forehead, knocked him unconscious, melted the metal on his clothing, and came out his right heel.

The 14-year-old Irving, Texas, boy was on third base in a local ball game when the lighting struck him. He lay on the ground 40 minutes while two policemen gave him heart massage and mouth-to-mouth resuscitation; then he was rushed to a hospital.

"I just think it wasn't my time to go yet," Greg said. "I knew it had to be more than luck that I lived. I guess the greatest feeling I had was when I walked out of that hospital. I could just as easy have been dead as alive."

Your time and my time could be any time. That's no cause to be morbid. But it's a good reason to be prepared.

We'll probably die the same way we live. Not a bad motive for starting today to be a little kinder, a little calmer, a little more patient and prayerful.

> "With him who fears the Lord it will go well at the end; on the day of his death he will be blessed."   [SIRACH 1:13]

✍ Remind me occasionally, Father, that my countdown has already begun.

THE UNITED NATIONS is pitting its World Health Organization against Africa's tiny blackfly.

WHO, one of the UN's 18 non-political agencies, is fighting the fly, the carrier of the vicious "river blindness" disease as part of a campaign against preventable loss of vision.

The agency is also combating three other major causes of blindness: trachoma, which thrives in unsanitary conditions; xerphthalmia, caused by lack of vitamin A; and glaucoma, controllable by early detection.

"Foresight prevents blindness," is the campaign slogan. If action is not taken now, says Joan Bush, WHO information officer, the world's blind people—now between 10 and 16 million—will double before the end of the century.

Another kind of blindness is even more widespread—and preventable, too—the inability to see another person's need. Have you ever "seen" when it's too late to help? Practice awareness today, now.

"Lord, let our eyes be opened."
[MATTHEW 20:33]

  Help me, Lord to open my eyes and my heart to others.

CHILDREN AND ADULTS who got together one summer in Kingston, New York, built more than a playground. They built a sense of respect for each other.

It was not a conventional see-saw playground. What the group of men and women and swarms of children worked on had ropes and painted tires, telephone poles, oil drums, mounds of dirt with places to climb and places to hide in.

Located near a small housing development and endorsed by local officials, this community project cost about $4,000, half the estimated amount.

"There's no reason why this can't be done throughout the country," said a local official.

"This'll stimulate your body," said one pleased 8-year-old. Another, aged 10, added: "And it'll keep us people out of trouble."

People living and working together for a common purpose is one way of describing a community. Is there something you and your neighbors can do to make your neighborhood more of a community?

"Love does no wrong to a neighbor; therefore love is the fulfilling of the law."
[ROMANS 13:10]

~§ Strengthen us, Lord, as we try to reach out and do something in the wider world.

WHAT DOES A TALENTED young stockbroker do when he loses his job? Richard DeNapoli decided to shine shoes.

The imaginative 30-year-old broker prepared a resume. Then he set up a shoeshine stand in Boston, passing out copies of it to each customer. One customer was a salesman for a map company in Detroit. Impressed, the salesman relayed Mr. DeNapoli's qualifications to his company, which hired him as southeastern Massachusetts representative for the firm.

Some people find a way to overcome difficulties that leave others merely complaining. They look to the future asking "What can I do?"—instead of grumbling over the misfortunes of the past.

Whether we succeed or not ultimately depends on how God disposes events. But He won't do our trying for us. That much we have to do.

Do you look ahead with action in mind, or seek refuge in "what might have been"?

"There is hope for your future, says the Lord."   [JEREMIAH 31:17]

⊷ Give us a sense of adventure, Lord, and help us keep in mind we were called to life.

UTHOR PAUL HINNEBUSCH, O.P., treasures his first royalty, paid in full on the spot. It was a penny his father gave him in appreciation of his first poem. He was five.

He tells of his profound sense of wonder one day on watching a snowfall. He found himself matching the gentle fall of the flakes with the rhythm of words and melody: "Winter out, snowing out, snowing on the porch roof." He repeated it again and again.

His father heard him and bestowed the penny, a token of his joy in and with his son. "In listening to my poem," recalls Father Hinnebusch, now a Dominican priest, "my father had listened to me . . . His loving attention and appreciation gave me a new sense of worth, and encouraged my mental and spiritual growth . . ."

So often we hear but don't listen. To listen to another is to go beyond words and actions to the reality inside. It takes caring, patience and awareness. Listen. You can plant a seed in a human heart.

"Be ready to listen."   [SIRACH 6:35]

   Lord, may we have the perception to listen for the voice within the other person.

NEW HAMPSHIRE WANTS ITS TOURISTS to slow down, enjoy their state more—and save lives.

Motorists driving on the Spaulding Turnpike will find a new type of rest stop—the Hilton Park-Safety Rest. There is more than the usual trashcans and restrooms. Hilton Park-Safety Rest is a 20-acre park and playground. It offers fishing, a boat dock, launching facilities, slides and swings, fireplaces and picnic tables.

Local school groups often visit the park-safety rest to observe the marine life and migratory birds.

Open from April until November, the facility is maintained by turnpike revenues. It offers an imaginative alternative to exhausted travellers.

There is so much of God's beauty to enjoy if only we slowed down. No matter where we're going—physically, emotionally or spiritually—getting there can be a lot of fun. If we let it. Are there any "park-safety rest" areas in your life?

"Come away by yourselves to a lonely place, and rest a while." [MARK 6:31]

✍ Jesus, You made room for quiet time in Your busy life. May we do so too.

ETIREMENT CAN BE A DREAM—or a nightmare—depending on how carefully those long-awaited hours of leisure are invested. These "investment tips" guarantee high returns in satisfaction:

■ Read to children, hospital patients or the blind.

■ Help organize an arts or crafts festival.

■ Babysit for families going through a major illness or other crisis.

■ Shop for shut-ins.

■ If you have a skill, share it by tutoring or becoming a volunteer teacher.

■ Be a foster grandparent at a child-care center.

■ If you're musical, organize a musical group to entertain nursing home residents.

■ Work with the League of Women Voters, or the political party of your choice.

What can one person do? One retired person—even with age-related health problems and limited income—can do many things. A little thought and "looking around" will suggest some.

"Look at what is before your eyes."

[2 CORINTHIANS 10:7]

ᴇ§ Holy Spirit, guide retired persons to find ways to make a difference in their world.

Howard Rice of Birmingham, Michigan, plans to spend the next two and a half years sailing around the world.

The 20-year-old man has set off alone on a journey aboard his homemade craft, the sailboat *Karsey Girl*, equipped with food supplies, a radio and homing device, and a harmonica to keep himself company.

The voyage is the first long one for Mr. Rice, who has set his course along the east coast of the U. S., through the Panama Canal, across the Equator to the Galapagos Islands, then to Tahiti, the Fiji Islands, past Australia, across the Indian Ocean, across the Atlantic to the east coast of South America and north to Florida.

"This is just something I've always wanted to do," said Mr. Rice. "It's going to be a slow trip, but why not do it?"

There is a restlessness in the human heart that some try to ease by travel. Why is it there? What does it mean? How can it be satisfied? These are questions worth thinking about.

"For the inward mind and heart of a man are deep!"　　[PSALM 64:6]

ᴇᔕ　Our hearts were made for You, Lord. Don't let us settle for less.

HOW DO YOUNGSTERS LEARN to enjoy reading? By starting early, say 20 top British educators.

"The best way to prepare the very young child for reading," say these specialists, "is to hold him on your lap and read aloud to him stories he likes—over and over again."

The secret, say the educators, is in the child's associating the printed page with physical comfort, security, a reassuring voice and the fascination of the story.

"All these combine," they report, "in the child's mind, to identify books as something which holds great pleasure."

Reading can be a lifetime joy and it needs to be encouraged. Anything you can do to assist young people to appreciate the treasures in the world of literature will be time well spent.

You might also suggest to capable persons thinking of a teaching career that they consider becoming specialists in teaching reading to slow learners.

"Take heed to yourself and to your teaching." [1 TIMOTHY 4:16]

  Give us a deeper love of learning, Lord, and the opportunities to share it with others.

Drivers who over-park in downtown Milwaukee may not find a $5 ticket awaiting them. Instead, they may find the meter has been fed another coin and this note left in an envelope on their windshield:

"You have just been rescued from a $5 parking ticket by the Robin Hood Public Parking Aid." The note asks the motorist to send $1 to help "Robin Hood" continue his service.

Milwaukee's modern-day Robin Hood is Bruce Vanier, a 23-year-old entrepreneur on a 10-speed bicycle who spots and feeds lapsing meters. Mr. Vanier has evidently found enough grateful drivers to fund his rescue operation, and the city attorney's office conceded that his philanthropy is not illegal.

In a world marked by a "me-first" attitude, there's something appealing about a man who puts coins in other people's meters. What have we done lately for somebody else?

> "Open wide your hand to your brother, to the needy and to the poor in the land."
> [DEUTERONOMY 15:11]

      Guide us to look more deeply, Jesus, at the ways in which You went about "doing good."

WHEN RESTAURANT OWNER Betty Sayles was a good Samaritan to a band of hungry young campers, her confidence was well rewarded.

After their van broke down in Saranac Lake, New York, during an Adirondack outing, a group of students were without money to meet the emergency. Bearded and unkempt after their trail experiences, they appealed to Betty Sayles of Betty's Restaurant. She trusted them and gave them their choice of anything in the cafe.

Soon afterward, Mrs. Sayles received a check for the amount of the students' bill, with a letter thanking her "for the kindness and trust you have shown to the members of the outing club." Said the letter's closing lines, "It is nice to know that there are still individuals that have faith and trust in our young people."

It's something to think about. Are we trusting persons? The way of trust is sometimes the way of disappointments, but it beats the alternatives of distrust, fear and rejection. Trusted anyone lately?

"I rejoice, because I have perfect confidence in you." [2 CORINTHIANS 7:16]

⋐ Give us more of the trusting attitude You show toward us, Lord.

A PRIEST IN COLOMBIA who spent a year as a garbage picker got a big helping hand from a Swedish Protestant Organization.

Vincent Mejia told an ecumenical meeting in Stockholm how he was helping unemployed people support themselves by scavenging for saleable refuse. He had organized a "dump cooperative," which enabled the men to get better prices for scrap materials.

"It may have been that the Gospel often has functioned as opium to the people and that the Church has been on the side of the rich," he told his audience of Baptist, Methodists and Pentecostals. "However, what I am just now experiencing is that the Gospel is also to make men free for a new life and a new hope."

Impressed, his hearers provided Father Mejia with materials he needed to continue and funds for building. The Gospel operates through deeds as well as words. Does it operate through you and me?

"Our gospel came to you not only in word, but also in power and in the Holy Spirit and with full conviction."

[1 THESSALONIANS 1:5]

Pat,

≥§ Remind us constantly to work together, pray together and love each other as Your children, Father of all. *Amen* ☺

227 / AUGUST 15, *1978   Vein stripping day . In memory of ---- from Judy*

FANS OF THE Books and Such Bookstore in Los Angeles may be the country's youngest militant consumer group.

When the store, which specialized in books for children only, cancelled its free Saturday morning storytelling hour to make way for the summer rush of book sale customers, the kids fought back.

Carrying placards that read "Unfair to Kids," "Stories, Not Sales" and "We Want Lindy's Stories," the youngsters marched determinedly around the entrance until co-owner Lindy Michaels came out to read to the young demonstrators.

For a long time, people have "taken things lying down." Now, even youngsters are increasingly demanding their rights, standing up for what they believe in.

On many levels, the consumer revolution is just beginning. Our country was founded on a legitimate protest. Let your voice be heard. Speak up for your rights and for the needs of the exploited.

Let business, labor, government, schools and other institutions know what you expect.

> "Out of the abundance of the heart his mouth speaks." [LUKE 6:45]

⤳ Help us acquire the wisdom to know what is best for us, Holy Spirit, and the energy to go after it.

IF YOU WANT TO REMEMBER things better, maybe these tips from writer Ted Pollack will help:

1. *Intend to learn.* List, at least mentally, what you'll gain by remembering.

2. *Be accurate.* Don't rush, take frequent breaks.

3. *Understand the material.* Never learn by rote.

4. *Look for the basic principles.* They are much easier to remember than specific examples.

5. *Make use of your present knowledge.* Look for something in what you already know on which to "hang" what you're trying to learn.

6. *Overlearn.* Continue to drill yourself—even after you think you've mastered the material. Repetition will help you remember longer.

A good memory is a definite asset. By remembering past successes, we can build on them. By remembering past failures, we can avoid repeating them. And one thing always worth remembering is that God has put us here to make a difference. How we do so is our decision.

> "If you will, you can keep the commandments, and to act faithfully is a matter of your own choice." [SIRACH 15:15]

ᴄᔕ Holy Spirit, may we remember who made us and why.

IN A GRUELLING NINE-HOUR TRIP around Connecticut by bus and train, Phyllis Zlotnick demonstrated travel problems of the handicapped.

Without help, she couldn't reach the ticket counter, get down the stairs to the platform, make a phone call, use the ladies room, get in or out of the station or fit the wheelchair in the bus.

"If there weren't attitudinal barriers," says Miss Zlotnick, "there wouldn't be architectural barriers. What good is housing and employment if we can't get there."

Things are looking up. Several cities are testing or already using buses designed for the handicapped. Others have a dial-a-ride minibus service. Chicago has a braille transit system guide.

When we consider them at all, most of us accept the problems of handicaped people as "the way it is." But the way it is, isn't the way it need be. Do you care enough to reject "the way things are" and do something about it?

> "Arise, for it is your task, and we are with you; be strong and do it." [EZRA 10:4]

    ❧ Help us, Father, to take on the job of trying to ease the burdens of the handicapped.

ITH A CORPORATE CHUCKLE, United Airlines, a few years ago, included in a newsletter these regulations set down in the 1920's for aircraft operators:

1. Don't take the machine into the air unless you are satisfied it will fly.

2. Pilots should carry hankies in a handy position to wipe off goggles.

3. In case the engine fails on takeoff, land straight ahead regardless of obstacles.

4. If you see another machine near you, get out of its way.

5. Do not trust altitude instruments.

6. Pilots will not wear spurs while flying.

7. If an emergency occurs while flying, land as soon as you can.

In less than half a century, those regulations sound as quaint as lace doublets and silver-buckled shoes. If you think things aren't changing fast, take a second look. Then, work and pray to keep the rush of events moving in a positive direction.

> "Let days speak, and many years teach wisdom." [JOB 32:7]

    Holy Spirit, give us wisdom amidst the rush of each day's happenings.

Getting away from it all for Tom and Gladys Johnston meant leaving the commercial advertising game in New York and building cliff dwellings on the Caribbean isle of Bequia.

The Johnstons have been there since 1961. With the help of local builders, they have made homes out of 16 caves with spectacular views of the sea.

"If I knew architecture, I wouldn't have put up the thing," Tom Johnson said of Moonhole, his first dwelling. It consisted of a series of rock and concrete chambers connected by stone catwalks and plazas. Profit is not the object. The Johnstons sell at reasonable prices to people they like.

Friends from the mainland bring them books for recreation. Instead of "turning into cabbages," as some people had feared, the Johnstons discovered that it was some industrialists who came to visit them who had "turned into cabbages."

What are we living for? The answer to that may indicate whether we feel like a cabbage or a king.

> "Before a man are life and death, and which-ever he chooses will be given to him."
>
> [SIRACH 15:17]

     Guide us, Jesus, in each step of life's journey.

THE RICH OF THE WORLD ARE "arguing about hunger on a full stomach," charges Filipina sociologist Gelia Castillo.

Speaking at the World Food Conference of 1976 at Iowa State University, Ms. Castillo urged the professionals attending the conference to dispense with lofty discussions of technological alternatives to world hunger and begin putting into action field projects "so that food may actually be produced rather than simply discussed."

Ms. Castillo expressed doubts that the rich could be committed to changing the lot of the poor, because, she noted, this would require a drastic change in the standard of living the rich themselves enjoy.

How much are any of us willing to scale down the way we live in order to raise the chances that somebody else may eat? More, perhaps, than the cynical may think. But there needs to be some assurance that what we do without will actually reach people in need.

And that requires political leadership of a high order.

> "But if any one has the world's goods and sees his brother in need, yet closes his heart against him, how does God's love abide in him?" [1 JOHN 3:17]

❧ Make us more aware that we are all dependent on one another, Father.

WHEN A CLOSING SUBWAY DOOR pulled his wedding ring from his finger, Frank Gittens imagined he would never see the ring again. But he was wrong.

Mr. Gittens had just come to New York from Trinidad. He was heartbroken over the loss of the ring. Meanwhile, inside the train, Shelly Ginis, 22, retrieved the ring and called the *New York Daily News*. She explained what had happened and gave the ring's inscription: Frank and Linda 7/16/72.

Mr. Gittens spotted the story in the News and called to claim his ring.

"She's very good," he said gratefully. "I'm new in this country. I think she's very nice. I would like to see her and thank her."

Stories like this one are a refreshing reminder that love of neighbor hasn't gone out of style. It also indicates where to find our neighbor—in the subway, the supermarket and anywhere else where one of God's children could use a helping hand.

> "Let each of us please his neighbor for his good, to edify him."   [ROMANS 15:2]

⊷ Father, open our eyes and our hearts to our neighbor's trouble.

Medical costs are high. Protect your pocketbook as well as your health, says the Council on Family Health, with these practices:

■ Read labels carefully; keep medicine in its original bottle.

■ Keep an accurate count of your daily dosage by measuring it out each morning for the day. Label the dosage. Take only recommended amounts.

■ Don't waste medicine and risk ineffectiveness by discontinuing its use because you feel better. Follow instructions or you may have to start over.

■ Save money by getting "starter" supplies of drugs from your physician.

■ Don't buy non-prescription drugs in large quantities unless really needed. Drugs deteriorate.

Good health is something money can't buy. And without it our energies can be greatly reduced. Those who want to be God's instruments in changing the world for the better do well to choose the ounce of prevention over the costly pound of cure.

"The Lord created medicines from the earth."   [SIRACH 38:4]

&ed; Father, may we cherish and preserve the gift of health.

P RISONER-VOLUNTEERS ARE FINDING new careers in working with seriously retarded men in Massachusetts' Fernald State School.

Through a program called CARVE (Concord Achievement Rehabilitation Volunteer Experiment) the men of Concord State Correctional Institution go daily by bus to Fernald, where they work from 8 to 4. An average of 16 volunteers serve as aides, providing physical care and engaging residents in activities.

While encountering a few problems, the four-year program has an over-all record of success. Most prisoners find in the work a way to contribute and feel useful, and in the process, develop self-respect,

Some become regular Fernald employees after parole, with over 50 percent working out well.

Such instances are gratifying signs that penal reform is possible. But the efforts of countless thousands will be needed to do the job nationwide. How can you translate into twentieth-century terms Christ's words: "I was in prison and you came to Me." (Matthew 25:36)

      Jesus, may more of us take up the cause of those who are all but forgotten.

SEVEN-FOOT HIGH CORN and fields of leafy greens now grace the once-bleak Hart Island in New York's East River. The 101-acre island is the site of five Phoenix House residences for rehabilitation of drug addicts.

John Feaghan, a 55-year-old resident who grew up on a farm in Ireland, had the idea. He heard that rising costs posed a problem in feeding the 350 former addicts. At his suggestion, potatoes and nine other vegetables were planted.

Jack Sacks, administrator of the five facilities, says the venture has cut costs by about 10 percent. By next year, says Mr. Sacks, ". . . all our Phoenix Houses in the city, which feed about 800 residents . . . will be self-sustaining as far as vegetables go."

John Feaghan took his experience—farming—and applied it to a problem—soaring food costs—in his community. You and I have experience; we live in communities; they have problems. With God's help, we can start making a few applications.

> "Imitate us . . . with toil and labor we worked night and day that we might not burden any of you." [2 THESSALONIANS 3:7,8]

> ✺ Holy Spirit, may we be creative in thinking of ways to find constructive solutions.

A SWEDISH-BORN PHOTOGRAPHER put together some scraps to provide his friends with the missing flag for a house-raising party and his life changed.

On that day, Anders Holmquist became a flag-maker. He designs and weaves the banners in his New York studio. Some are for organizations, but perhaps the most intriguing orders are those from individuals.

The flag-maker uses abstract designs, crowns, suns and other motifs. For artist Andrew Wyeth, he made a star in shades of blue on a black background. Color is important. He even gives people a color test to uncover personality.

"People today who order flags are seeking an expression of their identity," says Mr. Holmquist.

We don't really need a personal flag to express who we are. Our voices, the way we walk, our homes, our faces reflect us. Our attitudes and principles, or lack of them, affect even our small choices and radiate outward. What is the "you" that others see?

You are making some difference. What is it?

> "I will give you as a light to the nations, that My salvation may reach to the end of the earth." [ISAIAH 49:6]

୰ May we permit You to be the core of our lives, Lord, so the world may see You in us.

A NUN DISCOVERED two long-missing Italian masterpieces and gained $376,850 for her college.

The two works by Renaissance master Paolo Veronese had lain unnoticed at Salve Regina College in Newport, Rhode Island, since millionaire Robert Goelet left them, with his 50-room "summer cottage," to the diocese of Providence in 1947.

Then Sister Lucille McKillop, president of the college, asked for an estimate of the cost of cleaning the pictures. A dealer immediately offered $60,000 for the pair, and Sister McKillip consulted Hugh Hildersley of Sotheby Parke Bernet galleries.

"The paintings were in incredible, super condition," said Mr. Hildersley. "I had no doubt about it—these were two unknown Veroneses. They've never been catalogued and never been mentioned for centuries."

Treasures don't do much good until they're recognized. What interests or abilities has God placed in our keeping that we have yet to find—and put to use for ourselves and others?

> "The good man out of his good treasure brings forth good."   [MATTHEW 12:35]

   Grant us a greater discernment, Holy Spirit, of the treasures You have given us.

ONCE BLACK WITH SLUDGE, England's Thames River is now a model for pollution fighters everywhere.

The royal river, cleanest of all Europe's major waterways, has been the subject of an intense 15-year project which eliminated factory sewage drainage, increased oil spillage fines from $125 to $1000, introduced stringent sanitation laws for all boats and banned hard detergents in all of England.

"The river is healthy because the people wanted it that way," says L.B. Wood of the Thames Water Authority. "If you want clean rivers, you have to be willing to pay for them, and impose severe standards of enforcement."

The lesson of modern life may well be that there is no "cheap anything." Auto pollution control reduces mileage; replacement of land after strip-mining adds to the cost of coal; cleaning up waterways is slow, difficult and expensive.

But isn't the ability to do the right thing, especially when it is hard, a sign of maturity?

"We are to grow up in every way."
[EPHESIANS 4:15]

ᵫ§ Deepen our appreciation of the need to make honest choices in our lives, Lord.

A SICK CHILD WOKE A WHOLE TOWN to action for the plight of a group of migrant workers.

When Indiana's Associated Migrant Opportunities Service was called about a sick child, they found the child came from a camp unknown to county or state sanitarians. Eight families of tomato pickers huddled in two houses "without heating stoves, no showers, no hot water, one pump, one refrigerator and two outhouses in miserable, filthy condition."

Alerted by County Sanitarian David Faulkner, the nearby town of Greensburg gathered blankets, clothing, toys and food. A church bus took the migrants to the health clinic, and a dentist checked their teeth.

"It is an amazing story of community cooperation," said one official, "and one of the worst situations migrants have to put up with on the other hand."

Individual efforts are needed to help migrants. But legal action is also important. Only the force of law will assure basic decency and justice. How do your community and state treat migrant workers?

> "If you really fulfill the royal law, according to the scripture, 'You shall love your neighbor as yourself,' you do well." [JAMES 2:8]

> ❧ Make us more sensitive, Lord, to those in our midst who exist without life's basic necessities.

TWELVE DAYS IN THE Michigan wilderness taught three college students how to survive.

To show that getting lost need not be fatal, the three spent almost two weeks in Houghton Lake State Forest, sleeping on the ground and living on rodents they trapped, supplemented by boiled spiders, insects and wintergreen berry tea. Most nights the temperature dropped to zero.

Emerging healthy but much thinner, the three agreed that discipline of mind was the most vital factor in survival.

"You can die in the woods in one night," said the expedition's leader. "The first emotion that usually hits a stranded person is panic."

Panic can cause a lot of trouble—even if you're not lost in the woods. When crisis hits, try to pause—however briefly—to take stock of things. Include a brief prayer.

That won't make the problem go away. But it might help us get a handle on it.

"He reassured them and comforted them."
[GENESIS 50:21]

ᴇ§ Holy Spirit, even in moments of panic, may we remember Your love.

FLORIDA FOOD SALESMAN Jim Gillies doesn't believe in nursing homes for old people who don't need special care. At a Bible study course, he got an idea. Someone suggested that old people could live together like the early Christians, pooling resources. Mr. Gillies developed the idea into Share-a-Home.

A small group of elderly people live a family-like lifestyle with relative independence. They share expenses, including the salary of a manager, usually a couple, who run the household. Each group is a legally recognized family.

Now there are four homes in Florida overseen by the non-profit Share-a-Homes of America, Inc. "This is not a business proposition," says resident Dr. Harvey Peck, a 95-year-old retired economics professor. "This is a social proposition."

Social or business, it makes good sense to work together for the common good of all. Maybe your town could use "Share-a-Home." Maybe you can start the ball rolling.

"Share what you have." [HEBREWS 13:16]

₰ Holy Spirit, guide older people as they seek ways of taking care of their needs.

WEEKLY SERMONS AND MUSIC from two Atlanta churches go in to people who can't go out.

Two Baptist pastors tape their Sunday services. Volunteers with cassettes visit the homes of more than 60 persons during the week. They need not be church members. The churches provide tape machines for those who don't have them.

"We want them to know that someone cares about them," says Rev. Russell T. Barker, "and when they have spiritual and personal problems, sickness or death in their families, they can call on us."

It's not only the sermon. The visit itself has value, says Rev. Herbert L. Gibson. "This brings about a Christian relationship that is more important than any well-prepared message."

When we give something of value to another, we say that we care. When we give ourselves, we show that we mean it.

God's care for us is unceasing. Our concern for others is proof that we're getting His message.

> "Have the same care for one another. If one member suffers, all suffer together; if one member is honored, all rejoice together."
> [1 CORINTHIANS 12:25,26]

❧ Open our eyes and our hearts, Holy Spirit, to the many chances we have to give.

Things are looking up for handicapped people in New Jersey. New legislation provides:

■ that all buildings used by the public be equipped for handicapped persons;

■ that municipalities provide special parking spaces with room for maneuvering wheelchairs;

■ that sidewalks be sloped;

■ that absentee voting be allowed;

■ that handicapped children be allowed to attend classes in other states if special courses they need are unavailable locally.

The requirements also affect future construction and buildings undergoing major reconstruction.

State Senate President Frank Dodd says: "Building becomes a habit of design. It was a matter of changing attitudes. It doesn't cost any more . . ."

We tend to think money is necessary to remedy society's ills. Sometimes it is. But if attitudes can change, money and other resources are often easily found. How are your attitudes?

"The mind of him who has understanding seeks knowledge."   [PROVERBS 15:14]

   &§ Father, open our minds to include the needs of others.

Lt took a quarter of a century, but John Witmer can now go to sleep at night with a clear conscience. Mr. Witmer, who recently sent payment for a parking fine that was 25 years overdue, wrote this note to the city of New York:

"As a citizen of this country, it is my responsibility to pay whatever fines that have been imposed upon me, whether I was conscious or unconscious of wrongdoing."

The Tennessee farmer, a devout Mennonite, explained that the ticket was incurred when he and his wife were visiting the city on their honeymoon. Almost forgotten for years, the unpaid fine had occasionally nagged his conscience, until a friend advised: "If it bothers your conscience, pay it."

One thing money can't buy is a good night's sleep. But a clear conscience will surely help us rest better. If the "still, small voice" is prodding you, heed it. Then, asleep or awake, you'll be at ease with God, your neighbor and yourself.

"I always take pains to have a clear conscience toward God and toward men."

[ACTS 24:16]

 Holy Spirit, may we listen to the stirrings of conscience.

THE OLDEST VOLUNTEER FIREMAN in the country has decided to retire at age 87.

When John Opthof, of Wallington, New Jersey, started fighting fires, his firehouse had two handdrawn hose reels. Mr. Opthof has been an active fire-fighter for 61 years.

"He's always there," said a local police officer. "He'll go down and help pull a hose off a truck and handle traffic. He's an active guy . . . one of the best."

Why did he retire? Not because he wanted to. "They have a new ordinance limiting the age to 65," explains the spry octogenarian.

"And I'll probably still stick my nose into fires once in a while, too," he adds.

A lot of factors contribute to long life. Among them, satisfying work must rank high.

We can't all pick our ideal job, but we might put more of ourselves into the work we do. It could have benefits all around.

"In all your work be industrious."

[SIRACH 31:22]

∽§ Whatever our years, Father, help us to make them full of love and good works.

A GROUP OF 140 SCIENTISTS have challenged the 2,718-mile Congo River, which defeated explorer Henry Morton Stanley 100 years ago.

In 1874, Stanley's party had traveled 2,118 miles of the river in 999 days, but had lost 240 of the 354 people who started out. Logs tell of men dying of "fever, battle, murder, drowning, starvation and crocodiles."

The current expedition involves experts from dozens of countries, with specially built rubber boats, the latest medicines, a fleet of helicopters and Land-Rovers for constant back-up of the boats.

While charting the still largely unexplored river, the scientists will conduct studies in botany, archaeology, conservation and medicine. A major goal is to find the remedy for river blindness, caused by a fly-borne parasite, that has destroyed the sight of three million Africans.

The struggle against disease may never be completed. But each of us can play some part in improving ourselves and the environment that is our world.

"Show me the path of life."

[PSALM 16:11]

Help us maintain a positive attitude, Father, in the face of so many dangers to human life.

CITIZENS IN CHESTER COUNTY, Pennsylvania, were threatened with a 30- to 50-percent property tax increase. Mostly retirees, they decided to "fight City Hall."

After three meetings, they formed the Tax Action Committee, or TAC, which organized groups around the county and gained 5,000 signatures for petitions against the increase. Membership in TAC grew to over 4,000, and dues financed a suit against the reassessment. TAC then went after the county budget as wasteful. It backed independent candidates for controller and treasurer who won by 3-to-1 margins.

Nobody owns the government—nobody, that is, except the people. But it's not enough for citizens to take part in elections. Officials need to be watched, so that they carry out the public service they promised. Do you monitor your elected representatives? They're your servants.

> "He who looks into the perfect law, the law of liberty, and perseveres, being no hearer that forgets but a doer that acts, he shall be blessed in his doing."
>
> [JAMES 1:25]

&§ Put into our hearts, Lord, an awareness of our rights and our responsibilities.

A HOUSEWIFE IN SUBURBAN MINNEAPOLIS has mobilized 19 churches and hundreds of persons to provide emergency services to nearly 35,000 people.

When Madeleine Roche of Brooklyn Park, Minnesota, was asked by her parish council to assist people in the inner city, she agreed. But she also felt there were people in need in the affluent suburbs. This was the start of CEAP—Community Emergency Assistance Program.

Volunteers provide food, baby-sitting services, do home repairs and sometimes give out-of-pocket funds for people who don't know where to turn. Meals are prepared and delivered to elderly and handicapped persons. CEAP tries not to duplicate existing services, but to direct people to them.

Like other local groups springing up across the country, CEAP gets no government help. There are limits to what government can do. But there is almost no limit on what individuals can do to restore a sense of service to their neighborhoods.

> ". . . rendering service with a good will as to the Lord." [EPHESIANS 6:7]

> ❧ When we try to do something about the problems in our own communities, Lord, help us to persevere.

Swedes smoke only a third as much as Americans. But Sweden is launching the toughest anti-smoking campaign in the world.

The program will use all possible pressures to create a society in which smoking will never again be a major hazard to public health. To be included:

- Concentrated anti-smoking education.
- A ban on cigarette vending machines by 1979.
- A ban on sale of cigarettes anywhere but in tobacco shops.
- Outlawing of cigarette advertising.
- Use of movies and TV for do-not-smoke pleas.
- Annual price hikes (the price is now $1.50 a pack in Sweden).
- Gradual elimination of smoking in public places.
- A national drive to help smokers quit.
- Possible boost of insurance premiums for smokers.

It's pretty obvious by now that smoking is a health hazard. So if you smoke, do yourself a favor—quit. You'll not regret it.

> "Health and soundness are better than all gold, and a robust body than countless riches."   [SIRACH 30:15]

&ᴢ Jesus, may we preserve our health so we can serve others.

ALEX SCHNEIDER, 10, unwrapped a water-propelled plastic rocket and found it broken.

His mother, Iris Schneider, a psychologist, was angry and decided to do something.

She wrote a letter to the manufacturer, with a carbon copy to the supermarket chain where she had purchased the toy.

The manufacturer sent her a new one. But the chain went further. Its office of consumer affairs sent samples of the set to the company's own laboratory for testing and found that the rocket just didn't stand up. The chain discontinued the toy.

Mr. Schneider received a letter advising her of the action.

An issue doesn't have to be of cosmic proportions to be sufficient cause for action. What bothers you? Write to those who can do something about it. The welfare of little children and of big companies may hinge on small matters.

"Take trouble with details."

[2 MACCABEES 2:30]

   May we realize, Father, that small efforts, too, are a way to do something for a better world.

Each year, Kentucky's Louisville Courier Journal and Louisville Times Newspaper Company saves 85,000 trees (190 acres of prime forest) for America.

That amount of timber was used for the company's two daily papers before it began recycling newsprint. Coordinating a pickup, repulping and recycling program with its publishing and distribution, the company encourages readers to bundle and leave their used papers on the curb for pickup. The bundles are delivered to a paper processor and a de-inking plant, then manufactured for re-use.

The recycled paper costs the Courier-Journal and Times $3.50 more per ton than print paper from virgin timber. But the company absorbs the loss as a valuable trade-off in ecological benefits.

Picture the saving of newsprint as the saving of trees and woodland for future use. Find ways to conserve natural resources. Can you see the forest for the trees?

"Hold fast to what is good; love one another with brotherly affection."

[ROMANS 12:9]

≈§ Widen our vision, Holy Spirit, so that we may look deeply into those around us, and love them.

For Louis Milrod, receiving a master's degree at age 80 is just the beginning. He now plans to work for his Ph.D.

Mr. Milrod, the oldest person to receive a degree in Yeshiva University's 43rd annual commencement, says he looks forward to enrolling in New York University's doctoral program.

"Always during my life," he said, "the harder I worked the healthier I became. I'll just keep studying. It's good, very good."

Mr. Milrod did not complete his work for a high school diploma until he was 75.

Hard work doesn't always improve health, but if we have a purpose in what we do we'll probably do it better. And that's true whether we're young or old.

It would be a disservice to try to stop someone from working or going to school just because of age.

There's a lot to be said for being young in spirit. It's a quality, thank God, that has nothing to do with the number of years we've been around.

> "Speak to all who have ability, whom I have endowed with an able mind."
>
> [EXODUS 28:3]

&§ Fill us, Lord, with a desire to tell people what they can do instead of harping on what they cannot.

A FALL IN THE TUB LED Louis H. Ridgeway into a whole new venture—manufacturing soft bathtubs. Mr. Ridgeway's collision with his slick, hard tub gave him the idea for a tub that is both soft and long-lasting. Its outer layer of soft vinyl is bonded to a half inch of foam supported by fiberglass.

Mr. Ridgeway says the tub is almost impossible to slip in. "The foam is impact-absorbing. Your feet dig into it, but it is not enough to throw you off balance." The cushioning also acts as insulation to keep bath water warm longer.

The inventor's plastics and fiberglass company now has 16 employees producing the tubs.

It's the smart businessman who spots a need and moves to market a product to meet it.

How many times do we see a human need and respond to it?

"What can I do to help?" is a good question to ask. The answer may be something that can mean a lot to someone.

> "We know that in everything God works for good with those who love Him."
>
> [ROMANS 8:28]

~ Sharpen our awareness, Lord, of the possibilities all around us.

JOHN BURSTEIN WEARS HIS HEART on his sleeve—
and a lot of other things too—to teach youngsters
about good health.

Mr. Burstein, a 25-year-old drama graduate of Hof-
stra University, tours New York area schools as "Slim
Goodbody." He wears a body suit with stomach, bones,
muscles and intestines painted on it.

In lively, 45-minute song-and-dance performances,
Mr. Burstein works with a "partner," Really Reel, a
tape recorder with thick pink lips, orange nose and
yellow eyes that roll as the reels turn. Slim and Really
give lessons about keeping healthy.

Mr. Burstein's aim is to celebrate good health, not to
preach. "If kids learn to take care of themselves now,"
he says, "they'll always be more in touch with themselves."

Good teachers have always had a flair for the dramatic. Being "preachy" doesn't work. Being "real"
does. How authentic are we in communicating what
counts in our lives?

> "Let the word of Christ dwell in you richly
> as you teach." [COLOSSIANS 3:16]

    Fill us with the conviction, Lord, that dull-
    ness has nothing to do with being an effec-
    tive teacher.

Have you heard the one about the farmer in Kansas? A stranger saw a farmer leaning against a fence taking a mid-morning rest. He stopped and asked what kind of people lived up ahead.

"What kind were they where you're from?" the farmer asked.

"Terrible."

"Well, that's the kind live here," said the Kansan.

Another stranger came along and asked the same question. Again, the farmer asked about the people in the newcomer's own home town.

"Lovely people," came the response.

The farmer looked at him, glanced down the road and said, "That's the kind live here."

This story may be exaggerated. But it's point is valid—our attitudes and expectations help determine how people will react to us. But there's hope here. We can change our attitudes, alter our expectations. We can light a candle rather than curse the darkness.

> "He who loves his brother abides in the light."   [1 JOHN 2:10]

❧ Jesus, may we go around looking for good —not for trouble.

Retired teachers in Oregon are contacting isolated elderly persons by telephone.

Rachel Jackson, community service chairman for the Oregon Retired Educators Association, recruited members by telling them, "Here's your chance to help your fellow man and render a community service."

Volunteers in "Dial-a-Friend" make daily calls to older persons. They call them at the same time every day.

One 96-year-old woman who usually answered promptly failed to respond one morning. A neighbor was contacted, found the woman seriously ill, and rushed her to a hospital where she was treated successfully.

"This project is ideal for retired teachers," says Mr. Jackson. "No money is needed to start a similar project—just people who want to help others."

If you want to help others—and if you have a telephone—maybe you can "go and do likewise."

> "You shall love the Lord your God with all your heart . . . You shall love your neighbor as yourself."
>
> [MARK 12:30,31]

&s Jesus, may we be innovative in serving the needs of our communities.

PROFESSOR ABRAHAM MASLOW of Brandeis University, Waltham, Massachusetts, used to challenge his students with questions like: "Which of you is going to write the next novel?" and "Who is going to be a saint like Schweitzer?"

Confronted with such big ideas, the students would only blush, squirm and giggle. Then, the famed psychologist would assure them that he meant what he said.

"If not you, who will?" he demanded.

We each could ask that question of ourselves. Blind chance didn't put us here. A loving God did, as part of His plan for creation. We are not given to know the total design of God's masterplan.

But each day that dawns reveals a little of our portion of that plan. Each moment, God holds out a chance to be more, to achieve more. Each moment, He gives us what we need to respond to that invitation. We have what it takes. Will we use it? If we don't, who will?

"Put out into the deep."   [LUKE 5:4]

    ❧   God, help us to use each day to realize the best that is in us.

It took MARY THU 25 YEARS of persistence to become an American citizen. She made it at 87.

Nearly blind and deaf, the frail Chinese woman took the oath of allegiance in a special ceremony in Brooklyn, New York. She was applauded by 290 other immigrants.

Mrs. Thu, unable to meet requirements of reading and speaking English, had petitioned many times for citizenship since her family arrived from Hankow in 1949. Finally, under Section 312 of the Immigration Law, Mrs. Thu was accepted as a special exception because her sight and hearing are impaired.

"You have made great sacrifices to obtain this goal," Judge John Bartels told Mrs. Thu. "But no gift is as great as the precious gift of American citizenship."

We show our appreciation for citizenship by participating in the workings of government. Strengthen what is good in our nation. Correct what is defective. Pray for our leaders. Make sacrifices for the common good.

> "Let every person be subject to the governing authorities. For there is no authority except from God."   [ROMANS 13:1]

ᴇᔑ Assist us as we seek to serve our nation, Father, but remind us that You are Lord of all the world.

Ⱳ ATCH OUT FOR THE "RADIANT FRONT," warns Dr. Stanley E. Lindquist, professor of psychology at California State University, Fresno.

Dr. Lindquist directs the Link-Care Foundation, which serves religious workers who have emotional problems. "Christians sometimes try to give the impression that God's presence keeps us always on Cloud Nine, when we know we also have times of depression," he says.

The psychologist insists that the "radiant front" can be a form of dishonesty, damaging to the person affecting it, and harmful to others.

"God allows us to experience the low points of life," he says, "in order to teach us lessons we could not learn in any other way. The way we learn those lessons is not to deny the feelings but to find the meanings underlying them."

Sometimes we feel we are on a cloud, sometimes under it. Only by recognizing our true state of mind can we find the truth that sets us free.

> "Behold, You desire truth in the inward being; therefore teach me wisdom in my secret heart." [PSALM 51:6]

ᥱ§ Grant us the honesty to face the truth about ourselves, Father.

IT HAS BECOME the "in" thing for army officers in Ghana to raise rabbits.

Started several years ago by Newlove Mamattah, the effort is an attempt to make the west African country of 11 million more self-sufficient in food so as to import less and combat inflation.

"If you're an army officer and you don't raise rabbits," Mr. Mamattah said, "you're out of date." He proudly pointed out that Col. I.K. Acheampong, the nation's military ruler, is raising more than 200 rabbits.

Ghana produces over a third of the world's cocoa, but much foreign exchange goes out in payment for corned beef, sardines, tuna and mutton from abroad. "Operation Feed Yourself" has produced about 30,000 rabbits for a national breeding stock.

As nations become independent, self-reliance is hard to achieve. In our own lives, it's the same. Ask God for help to pull your own weight, so that you can lend a hand to others as well.

> "Let him labor . . . so that he may be able to give to those in need."
>
> [EPHESIANS 4:28]

 ⁕ Grant us strength to carry on, Lord, and not become overly dependent on others.

WOULD WE BE HAPPIER if we learned from children? Yes, says Dr. Thomas Finch, an educator who maintains that theirs is a world of honesty, trust and love.

"They are down to the basics," he says. "They see the world as it is and enjoy it."

He offers these tips for becoming childlike:

1. Uncomplicate your life; be open and honest.

2. Don't be afraid to admit, "I can't do that" or "I don't know."

3. Don't hide your feelings or be afraid to show affection.

4. Delight in simple things.

5. Enjoy being you. Know who you are, what you can do and what is expected of you.

6. Don't hold grudges; let the past be past.

Children may not always be the "little angels" described by Dr. Finch. But there is much that can be learned by observing them. That's probably one reason Jesus told his followers: "Unless you turn and become like children, you will never enter the kingdom of heaven."   [MATTHEW 18:3]

    *§ Holy Spirit, teach us how to be truly and healthily childlike.

IN A COMPUTER AGE, the human memory is still a little-understood mystery. Some of the facts science has unearthed about it are these:

■ The brain, with 10 billion working parts, has storage capacity for 10 new facts each second.

■ In a 70-year lifetime, a human stores information equivalent to one trillion words.

■ No human, even a genius, uses more than about one hundredth of the brain's capacity to store knowledge.

■ Nearly 10,000 thoughts pass in and out of the human mind each day.

■ The brain has no single memory storage area. Up to half the brain can be removed without memory loss.

■ After age 35, about 100,000 brain neurons are lost each day. The best way to keep memory sharp is through mental activity.

It's been said that "a mind is a terrible thing to waste." And it's a wonderful thing to use. Use it. Develop it. Tackle a new problem. Your mind—and your heart—can make this world a better place.

> "He made for them tongue and lips; He gave them ears and a mind for thinking."
>
> [SIRACH 17:6]

✑ Never let us neglect our abilities, Father. They are Your gifts.

BELVA COTTIER OF SAN FRANCISCO is a Sioux Indian who was raised on a reservation just 16 miles from Wounded Knee, South Dakota.

She remembers her grandfather saying, "You young ones go out and notify the people we're going to have a feast." They would signal with mirrors to people several miles away, "What do you have to share?"

To the American Indian, any feast, at any time, becomes an opportunity to share and give thanks, says Ms. Cottier. Director of the Native American Health Center for needy Indians and others, she speaks of the poverty among Indians today and admits that some of them question what there is to be thankful for.

Yet, she says, it is the Indian philosophy not to dwell on hatred or past wrongs.

It is difficult to give thanks with untroubled heart when so many have so little. Look around now for chances to make things right for someone, to fill a need, to share our plenty. It's a very practical way of saying "Thanks."

> "He who has two coats, let him share with him who has none; and he who has food, let him do likewise." [LUKE 3:11]

જ Lord, make us aware of others' needs—of the body and of the spirit.

WHEN STOREKEEPER SAM COHEN retired, Pittsburgh lost its most unusual specialty store.

For 60 years, Sam's store has sold nothing but umbrellas. It was the city's only umbrella store, and it never had a competitor.

His success centered on one thing, said Sam: "Catering to one item. I've carried 15,000 umbrellas in here. I always had what people wanted, any color, any size, any style. I know umbrellas from A to Z. The people at the department stores would tell customers, 'Well, Sam has it.' Sure enough, Sam would have it. That's always made me feel good."

When it comes to umbrellas, Sam Cohen knew what he was talking about. On what subjects can we speak with knowledge?

Listen to yourself today. Do you give the impression that you know everything about everything? Or do you hold back when you have an idea?

Somebody may be waiting for what we have to say —so we'd better know what it's all about.

> "If you utter what is precious and not what is worthless, you shall be as My mouth."
>
> [JEREMIAH 15:19]

  ◆§   Help us use our brains, Holy Spirit, in a way that will show we value what you've given us.

"**G**O BACK TO SCHOOL," says *Modern Maturity* magazine. You'll have an opportunity to stay "with it" and stay interesting. You'll have contact with others. You'll have fun.

The magazine suggests to older students:

1. Have your hearing and vision checked regularly and have appropriate corrections made. You may eliminate some learning problems.

2. Don't miss any classes. If you can't avoid doing so, get the missed assignment and make up the session immediately.

3. For better learning, study when well rested.

4. Give yourself plenty of time. You may be slow at first.

5. Keep an open mind and be flexible. New ideas and methods may be better than you thought.

An increasing number of people are now making education a lifetime pursuit. It's a praiseworthy decision. Learning isn't meant to stop on graduation day.

"Let days speak, and many years teach wisdom."   [JOB 32:7]

  ‣ Father, may we constantly develop our minds to better serve You.

267 / SEPTEMBER 24

THERE'S HOPE FOR TINY VICTIMS of malnutrition. Normal family life, scientists find, can reverse many of its bad effects.

It had been thought that early malnutrition permanently damaged brain development. To test this theory, Dr. Myron Winick of Columbia University's Institute of Human Nutrition studied Korean orphans adopted by American families.

He found that brain damage, though real, is largely overcome by adequate nourishment, loving care and intellectual stimulation provided in a normal family environment.

"The child who was malnourished may not reach his full ultimate potential," says Dr. Winick, "but at least we now know he can come out normal."

Malnutrition's damage need not be devastating. But need there be damage at all? There will be until enough of us choose to "feed the hungry." Do something.

"I was hungry and you gave Me food."
[MATTHEW 25:35]

   ❧ Father, may we not be discouraged by the enormity of hunger in the world, but help one person to eat.

T HE MOST SUCCESSFUL THERAPIST at Ohio's Castle Nursing Home is not a psychologist or a social worker. It's a dog.

A specially bred German shepherd, Whisky, is part of an Ohio State University experiment in "pet-facilitated psychotherapy." Already he has helped a mute patient to speak his first words in 26 years, and coaxed a 65-year-old patient to eat after a 27-day fast.

Don De Hass, Castle's administrator, says Whisky and other dogs produce remarkable results with withdrawn patients by filling their need to feel worthwhile to themselves and others. Says Mr. De Hass:

"Patients can accept the love of an animal more easily than that of a human. The pet doesn't criticize, but accepts the person as is and gives love freely."

Humans have the responsibilities that some pets fulfill. We could all stand improvement when it comes to giving acceptance and love. To be a caring person is worth prayer—and effort.

"Love is patient and kind."
[1 CORINTHIANS 13:4]

₷ Keep us aware of the fact that how we show love, Lord, is the most important thing we do.

WRITING BETTER BUSINESS LETTERS can be easy if you follow these tips, says writer Ted Pollak:

■ Organize your thoughts before you start. Know what you want to say.

■ Speak to your reader. Use the "you" approach.

■ Be clear. Be brief. Be specific. Use short words and sentences limited to one idea each.

■ Be forceful. Write with a certain response in mind, and work to get it.

■ Write as you talk, without cliches or stilted phrases. Be informal. Then read your finished letter aloud to see if it sounds like you.

The marketplace isn't the only area that stands to benefit from more effective communication. Letters to the editor, to government officials and even friendly notes could use a little sprucing up, too.

One way to restate the Golden Rule is: "Correspond as you would be corresponded with."

"By your words you will be justified, and by your words you will be condemned."
[MATTHEW 12:37]

❧ Jesus, may our love for others shine through every thought, word and deed.

A NINE-TERM CONGRESSMAN spent a recent recess slinging hash, collecting garbage, delivering newspapers and pumping gas.

Ken Hechler of West Virginia gave this as his reason: "I was disgusted with the fact that Congress voted itself a pay raise and then voted for a month-long recess. I voted against both."

Mr. Hechler, 61, offered free help to anyone who would give him a job. He is well known in his district for his opposition to unrestricted strip-mining and for traveling around the mountains to visit constituents in his bright red jeep emblazoned with the words: "Ken Hechler. Your servant in Congress."

If more government officials slung hash, would they give people better service? Nobody knows. But it seems clear that those who get away from the feelings and needs of ordinary people are not doing their jobs.

Government of, by and for the people will last only as long as the people keep their eye on government.

"Like the ruler of the city, so are all its inhabitants." [SIRACH 10:2]

Give us a greater interest in government, Lord, so that we can think and speak intelligently on public matters.

THERE WAS NOTHING FISHY about the contents of the bag that Japanese fishmonger, Sanae Sato, found. It contained 90 million yen ($30,000).

Earlier in the day, the driver of a bank van told police he had been delivering money from one bank to another and, at his destination, the money bag was missing.

A patrol car checked the one-mile route without success. Ten minutes after their return, the fishmonger rushed into the police station with a canvas money bag. "Look what I found in front of my shop," he said. "I thought it was a bag of rice or a bundle of books."

The police said Mr. Sato will receive a "generous percentage" of the money as a reward.

Honesty like Mr. Sato's is refreshing. If the rest of us keep our dealings with each other "on the level," we can also make honesty more common. In Tokyo or Tacoma, an honest world starts with each one of us.

"Act honorably in all things."
[HEBREWS 13:18]

ℕ Father, may we be honest even when tempted to cut corners.

KARNS, CORBETT AND KISSANE is like any other struggling young law firm—with one difference. The three founding partners have been confined to wheelchairs since they were teenagers.

The three men met as undergraduates at the University of Pittsburgh, became friends, and went on to graduate from Pitt's Law School.

"We look at our handicap as an inconvenience. Given more time and more effort, we can accomplish the same as anyone else," says Mr. Kissane.

"The capacity of law does not involve the capacity to walk, but the capacity to think," says Mr. Karns.

"We don't see anything melodramatic in this," claims Mr. Corbett. "It's all a matter of living. It's all very simple. You have to answer just one question—whether you want to continue living. After that, there's no looking back."

Many people face crises when they wonder whether it's worthwhile to keep on living. May they heed the Bible's urging: "Choose life, that you and your descendants may live."   [DEUTERONOMY 30:19]

    Father, may our faith in You strengthen us in moments of trial.

PHILADELPHIA'S OLDEST CITY EMPLOYEE gave up a pool hustler's life at age 80 to help the elderly.

William Henry Burgess, now 84, spent years earning his living with a cuestick. Now he works for the Senior Citizens Friendship Corps visiting elderly shut-ins and helping them shop and clean house.

Each morning, Mr. Burgess receives a schedule for the day, with names and addresses of people to see. He visits each, chats awhile and finds ways to be useful.

"What do I talk about? It depends on what kind of life they've lived," says the lively octogenarian. "Wherever I go, they like me. I'll always be young."

Some people are "young" at 84. Others are "old" at 24. That's because age is as much a question of outlook as it is of birth date.

Relish new ideas, stay flexible in the face of constant change and ask God for the courage to take a few risks. If you do, your years—no matter how many— will weigh lightly on you.

> "God is our refuge and strength . . . we will not fear though the earth should change."
> [PSALM 46:1,2]

⋅⋅⋅ Father, teach us to take each day as a gift from Your hands.

WANT TO CHECK OUT A FROG from the library? If you lived in Teaneck, New Jersey, you could.

Donna Margulies's kindergarten lending library has shelves stocked with ferns, flowers, iguanas, mice, birds and frogs. Her 50 students may, with parental consent, take home a specimen for two or three weeks, after learning how to feed and care for it. Another requirement is a carefully kept daily log of the plant or animal's development, habits, or growth.

"I want children to be aware of how plants reproduce and how many varieties there are," says Mrs. Margulies. "Parents always want to be very much included. They, of course, have to do the writing," she adds.

We can introduce all kinds of technology and innovative teaching methods into our schools. If they are sound, everyone gains. But, dedicated, creative teachers are the most important part of any school system. Encourage them. Support them. And, once in a while, thank them.

"Truly teach the way of God."
[MARK 12:14]

❧ Holy Spirit, guide those entrusted with the education of our children.

REMEMBER THE SAYING, "There's no such thing as a free lunch"? Well, it's not so at Ries Cappiello Colwell. That New York advertising agency provides free lunch for all its employees.

Jack Trout, president, says he felt "it would be a nice move for our employees if we gave them lunch."

Another executive says it was done to save time and money consumed in two-hour business lunches.

Whatever the reason, the firm claims it's economical. "We get our money back in terms of increased efficiency," says one partner.

And the employees like it. "It's like coming home to mother," says one. "It puts your head at ease," claims another.

The business of business may be business. But there's no reason why good human relations can't be part of the package. And oddly enough, in the long run, good human relations often turns out to be good business, too.

"Those who plan good have joy."
[PROVERB 12:20]

   Jesus, You put people first. May we do likewise in our dealings with one another.

A DAY-CARE TEACHER sent this to us:

"Eight of us are in poetry reading. We . . . decided to make our poetry reading center around animals. We all wrote—everyone wrote a line.

Teacher: Dear Lord, help me to realize that I am not the only animal in God's creation.

Penny: We get homesick—teach us, therefore, not to separate any animal from its mother.

Maria: Teach us to be like our fellow creatures who hear through the silence and see through the darkness.

Robin: Teach us not to be angry at those creatures who steal from our plenty . . .

Allison: Help us to realize that skunks don't like the way we smell.

All: Thank you God for all your creatures—who keep us company on this lonely planet. Amen."

By respecting animals we check our own egotism and show respect for our better instincts. Life would be very different without them.

"I will remember My covenant which is between Me and you and every living creature." [GENESIS 9:15]

⧉ Lord, may we show children how to love by the way we ourselves love—both animals and people.

OUR ANCESTORS OF 50,000 YEARS AGO buried their dead on beds of branches and fresh flowers.

The body of a Neanderthal man who had been buried this way was found recently in a cave in the Iraq highlands, some 250 miles from Baghdad. Identification of the kind of flowers used pinpoints June as the month of his death. The interment took place between 50,000 and 60,000 B.C.

The Neanderthal people are believed to have lived over vast regions of Europe, western Asia and Africa until they became extinct about 35,000 years ago.

These ancient humans have passed into oblivion. But they have left behind mute evidence of their concern for the individual after death.

To be human is to know that we must die, and to choose how we will regard that final event of life. How we live today decides how we will complete our passage. May yours be a life with a happy ending.

> "Be faithful unto death, and I will give you the crown of life."   [REVELATIONS 2:10]

&ந Holy Spirit, point our lives toward God.

A North Dakota man got the idea of putting coded confetti in grain to discourage thieves. It works. James Cussons started the Grain Identification Company to print registered numbers on bits of paper.

Five pounds of the confetti—290,000 pieces—mix with 40,000 bushels of any grain. It positively identifies the owner, is inexpensive, and is easily removed by milling companies.

Piles of grain have been found near bins, indicating that thieves had noticed the "branding" and dumped it. "It's the greatest deterrent there is," says Sheriff Leroy Lutz. The previous year about 17 cases of grain theft had been reported in the area. "Now," he says, "we have no complaints at all."

The lure of something-for-nothing has wide appeal, though most of us manage to resist it. Fear of getting caught isn't the highest reason for being honest, but it helps. Don't make it easy for anybody, including yourself, to cut corners.

> "You shall not steal, nor deal falsely, nor lie to one another." [LEVITICUS 19:11]

> Help us, Lord, to take that little bit of larceny out of our hearts and replace it with a generous spirit.

A CHRISTOPHER FRIEND wrote this question about maturity: "What about the very important reminder of Jesus: 'Unless you be as little children, you shall not enter the Kingdom of heaven?' "

There's no doubt that Jesus required maturity of His followers—to carry their crosses; to seek justice; to accept persecution for the faith; to persevere to the end.

By urging us to be "as little children," He meant as St. Paul explained, "to be babes as regards evil." To become responsible, believing adults, it is not necessary to lose the winning qualities of children—lack of self-consciousness, playfulness, trust.

As our friend put it: "Perhaps He means for us to be both, perhaps each in its place."

To maintain a balance between "growing up" and maintaining the outlook of a child as not easy. But neither is following Jesus Christ. Alone, we couldn't do it. But, He assured us we wouldn't be alone. His help is there for us.

"In paths they have not known I will guide them."   [ISAIAH 42:16]

❧ May we grow in wisdom and knowledge, Jesus, while remaining open to the joys of life.

P APERS, BOTTLES AND CANS are recycled. Why not recycle schools?

Nassau County Planning Commission in Long Island, New York, projects a drop in public school enrollment from 326,000 in 1970-71 to 179,500 at the end of the next decade. Schools will be major tax burdens. At the same time, points out architect Sigmund Spiegel, there is a mounting need for moderate income housing for older people.

Mr. Spiegel has put it all together in a proposal that calls for conversion of surplus school buildings into housing. One plan calls for turning an unused East Meadow school and its 11-acre grounds into 328 garden apartments for older people.

Auditoriums, kitchens, etc., will become areas for arts and crafts and social activities.

As we come to realize that our resources are finite, more ideas are needed to make additional use of what we have. Conservation is everybody's business.

"Everything has been created for its use."
[SIRACH 39:21]

   ⋙ Spur in us the habit of thinking in terms of saving the resources, Father, You have put at our disposal.

YOU CAN NOT ONLY FIGHT CITY HALL, says Herbert Miller of the Georgetown University Institute of Criminal Law and Procedure, but you can win.

Mr. Miller gives these suggestions for effective citizen action:

- Join a community group that wields power.
- Be prepared to spend time.
- Look for real community issues—not abstractions.
- Form coalitions with groups sharing your views.
- Avoid forming a permanent organization. Organize on an issue; don't organize to organize.
- Beware of being co-opted into accepting minimal change. If you can, hire a lawyer to help.
- Keep the media well informed.

Many a good cause died because its parents didn't know how to raise it. People who want to bring about a more honest world need know-how that is on a par with their high goals.

You can change the world—at least a little—provided you go about it systematically.

"The people who know their God shall stand firm and take action." [DANIEL 11:32]

Make us tough-minded optimists in seeking to make living conditions better for ourselves and others, Lord.

HOW THE RECORD-BOOK GOT STARTED

A HOBBY OF COLLECTING out-of-the-way facts turned into the world famous *Guinness Book of Records*.

Started in 1955 by identical twins Norris and Ross McWhirter for the Guinness Company, the book lists thousands of bizarre superlatives, from the world's longest moustache (44 inches) to the strongest man (Paul Anderson, who lifted 6,270 pounds in 1972). Each year, 700,000 curious people buy the book.

"All over the country in 60,000 pubs people are arguing," says Norris McWhirter, "so they turn to us. We also get scores of letters asking us to settle bets."

What makes this book of unusual accomplishments so popular probably has something to do with our desire to see the outer limits of human achievement. We may feel that, if other people can do it, so can we.

The desire to excel can produce good results. And not just in physical exploits. It can lead to acts of kindness, perseverance and public service. There's a lot of love we can give the world, if we will.

"Aim at righteousness, godliness, faith, love, steadfastness, gentleness."

[1 TIMOTHY 6:11]

Give us the desire to be record-breakers, Jesus, in the work of comforting people in need.

STEEPLEJACK DON KUTZ finds it more relaxing swinging from a rig 250 feet above the ground than teaching sixth and seventh grade students.

Swinging from heights is not new in the family. The Natchez, Mississippi, man learned something of the steeplejack's craft from his father. When his father died, Mr. Kutz left his teaching career of 11 years to carry on the family trade of maintaining church steeples and clocks.

But he had another reason to switch—in order to calm his nerves. The hassle in the classroom was a threat to his equilibrium. Working aloft where he can see miles of tranquil countryside is making a new man of him.

"My nerves have calmed down," says Don Kutz. "It's a carefree life."

Getting perspective can calm us, although becoming a steeplejack may not be everybody's bag.

Pull back. Slow down. Let things settle. Let God do something. It's His world.

"To set the mind on the spirit is life and peace." [ROMANS 8:6]

   Grant us some long-range vision, Jesus, so we won't get tangled in the here-and-now.

S HORTLY BEFORE HE DIED, Admiral Samuel Eliot Morison, 87, published a book called, "The European Discovery of America: The Southern Voyages, 1492-1616."

The period starts with Columbus's first voyage and ends with the first sighting of Cape Horn. In that time a vast new world was discovered and partly explored; the globe was circumnavigated for the first time; the four colonial empires begun.

At 2:00 a.m., October 12, 1492, Columbus and a seaman sighted land. "Not since the birth of Christ," says Admiral Morison, "has there been a night so full of meaning for the human race."

But that was the beginning of a world realizing that it was only half a world, that another hemisphere existed, peopled with heretofore unknown human beings.

The empire builders have retreated. We are their successors. We make decisions in our jobs, as parents, as teachers, as members of the community, at the polls. Those choices are already building the world of tomorrow.

"Let us choose what is right; let us determine among ourselves what is good." [JOB 34:4]

꒖ May I have the perspective, Father, to see my life in the larger context of the human community.

VOLUNTEERS WORKING WITH PROBATIONERS have a news-letter, the *VIP Examiner*. A recent issue suggested that workers ask themselves these qustions:

1. Can I be—in some way which will be perceived by the other person—trustworthy, dependable, consistent?

2. Can I let myself experience positive attitudes toward this other person—attitudes of warmth, caring, liking, interest, respect?

3. Can I let myself enter fully into the world of his feelings and personal meanings and see these as he does?

4. Can I perceive him as he is? Can I communicate this attitude?

5. Can I act with sufficient sensitivity in the relationship that my behavior will not be perceived as a threat?

Try asking yourself these questions. They form a blueprint for caring. They could apply to a son or daughter, a spouse, a parent, a friend, a pupil. . . . .

> "This is the commandment we have from Him, that he who loves God should love his brother also."   [1 JOHN 4:21]

✑ Help me, Lord, to care enough to go past my own barriers of selfishness and apathy to reach others.

THREE OUT OF EVERY FIVE PERSONS polled could not name a single action performed in the past year by those who directed the nation's second largest enterprise, after defense—its public schools.

Public apathy and lack of confidence were the dominant themes of a recent report by the National School Boards Association. Boards in the smallest communities, especially in the south and midwest, received the highest marks for trying to keep the public informed.

Harold V. Webb, director of the Association, warned that "the nation's school boards generally are a barely visible government," a situation he considered unhealthy.

One of the nation's 16,738 school boards is in your town or neighborhood. Who are the members? What policies do they pursue? Do you agree? If not, what do you intend to do about it? Have you thought of running for the board yourself?

> "But let each one test his own work, and then his reason to boast will be in himself alone and not in his neighbor."
>
> [GALATIANS 6:4]

  Holy Spirit, bring us to a greater awareness of our responsibility to uphold the public interest.

A TAXI THAT HAS TRAVELLED 850,000 miles may reach a million before its owner retires it.

When he was a New York cabby, Robert Bender bought a 1956 Cadillac with 40,000 miles on it. Now, 14 years later, Mr. Bender uses the still-shiny auto as a cab in Madison, Wisconsin. He gets up at 4 a.m. each day to wash it with cold water. So far the car has needed only a few minor repairs, a new transmission and a paint job.

"I've seen the clock go around eight times," said Mr. Bender, who wears a blue chauffeur's uniform to add a touch of class to his job, "and I figure it will go around a couple more."

In a nation that's being called the "throwaway society," Robert Bender is a welcome exception. Good engineering helped his cab last. But so did his care and effort. If enough of us acquire a similar attitude, we'll greatly reduce the strain on the riches of God's good earth.

"The earth is the Lord's and the fullness thereof." [PSALM 24:1]

    ಆ§   Father, may we learn respect for the things we use.

T HE BLIND MAKE UP one of the newest militant minorities. They are tired of being treated, in the words of Edwin Lewinson, a history professor, "as being physically helpless and mentally retarded."

To counter discrimination from employers, landlords, etc., they now have a voice in the National Federation of the Blind (membership 50,000).

There are more individual voices, too. A suit brought by a teacher forced the Denver school district to affirm that blind and sighted job applicants would have equal treatment.

The Pennsylvania Human Rights Commission ordered a Philadelphia landlord to offer an apartment to complainant Henry Mitchell, a sculptor, and his guide dog.

It's easy to forget that the blind—and other handicapped persons—are often subject to arbitrary and unfair treatment. May God help us to think of them more often, to put ourselves in the place of other persons and to give them the same regard we want for ourselves.

> "So whatever you wish that men would do to you, do so to them."   [MATTHEW 7:12]

> Give us an expanding awareness, Jesus, of the potential in people, far and near.

You DON'T USE COINS for one jukebox at Albany Medical College. And you don't get music. You get education.

A medical student punches in the number of his selection and sits down to take notes. A nurse consults it for help with a difficult patient. A doctor stops to see what's current.

There are 160 five- to 10-minute selections, plus a slide projector to illustrate the instruction. Questions can be submitted to a tape recorder for later response.

What started out as an aid to physicians in their postgraduate education is also providing refresher courses and information on new medical developments.

"It doesn't take much imagination to imagine other possibilities," says Dr. Frank M. Woolsey. "Patient education, for example."

New methods of education open the possibility for lifetime learning on a broad scale. Do we want to keep growing in knowledge? Are we willing to make the effort? Such questions are worth study.

> "If you love to listen you will gain knowledge, and if you incline your ear you will become wise." [SIRACH 6:33]

> ⊷ Keep us alert, Lord, to every chance we have to grow in wisdom and knowledge.

IN BERGEN COUNTY, NEW JERSEY, when two pairs of women lawyers formed partnerships, both supporters and detractors called them "feminist law firms."

But all four women claim they just want to practice good law. In fact, Abraham and Stark, as it happens, has mostly male clients; while Meyer and Scharff has more women.

Each woman had entered law school after marriage and children. Each found that partnership with another woman allowed greater flexibility for personal needs.

"We put in the same number of hours as we would any place else," says Mrs. Abraham. "However, we do it in a way that conforms with the rest of our lives."

The Women's Movement has forcefully made the point that people need not be locked into a rigid job time-table with strictly defined roles. Personal needs can be met. For emphasizing that flexibility, we all owe the movement a debt of thanks.

> "I can do all things in Him who strengthens me." [PHILIPPIANS 4:13]

✎ Father, may we be creative in working out our lifestyles.

For five hours, 53 shipwrecked Bahamians clung to a tiny, wave-swept rock island until U.S. Coast Guard helicopters rescued them.

The men, women and children were passengers and crew of the Bahamian inter-island freighter San Salvador Express, which ran aground 27 miles out of Nassau. Everyone aboard managed to cluster on the 20-by 30-foot rock island to await rescue.

"If there had been a storm, they would have been in even more trouble," said helicopter pilot Jan Long. "As it was, no boat was able to get in there. They were awful glad to see us."

Lt. Commander Long landed his helicopter on a coral outcrop and some passengers swam out to meet him. He carried 24 to safety. A second pilot rescued 29 elderly passengers and children.

How precious life is comes through in accounts of daring rescues. But what about life in the womb, the prison cell, the battlefield or the invalid's bed?

It's precious there too. Are you a lover of life?

> "Therefore choose life . . . loving the Lord your God, obeying His voice."
> [DEUTERONOMY 30:19]

ᴇᴥ§ Father, let us learn to cherish Your most precious gift.

Thirteen Indiana college students wound up behind bars in the Jasper County Jail—and paid tuition for the experience.

The students, taking a course called "Juvenile Delinquency: A Search for Meaning," were jailed overnight as a class assignment. Said their instructor:

"I'm trying to get their noses out of books, to give my kids a taste of real life."

Each student had a separate cell, where he was placed after being searched and deprived of all possessions. One freshman summed up the experience:

"Being left alone like this all night, now I can see what it would be like for a delinquent during his first arrest."

It's not likely that a single night in jail under these conditions can begin to convey the desperation of the real thing. But it can help.

In any field, a purely theoretical approach is usually inadequate. We need understanding. Experience is one way to get it.

> "Buy wisdom, instruction and understanding." [PROVERBS 23:23]

&§ Spur us to combine a respect for ideas, Holy Spirit, with a closer knowledge of things in the concrete.

Benjamin Franklin's life gives the lie to the widely held belief that a person can be too old to perform a useful service.

When he was 70, Franklin was given the difficult commission of negotiating with France for economic and military assistance to the United States.

While in France, he created the American navy, arranged for financing for the revolution and presided in prize courts.

Franklin was 72 when he worked out the treaty of alliance with France, which put victory and independence within reach.

At 76, he negotiated the peace treaty with Great Britain. He was 81 when he organized America's first anti-slavery society.

Failing health and incapacity can sharply limit what we do. But it is wrong to think that age alone is reason to put people on the inactive list. At any stage of life, thank God, while we cannot do everything, we can do something.

> "Go, do all that is in your heart; for the Lord is with you." [2 SAMUEL 7:3]

> ✍ Make us think of others—and ourselves—Lord, in terms of what we can do, not what we can't.

FOR A FEW MINUTES, 3-year-old Chip Gunn became a young man with a mission.

The Atlanta youngster was playing at home when his mother fell to the floor in excruciating pain. Unable to reach the phone, she managed to summon Chip and sent him for help to a neighbor.

"I told him to hurry, but really didn't know what he would do because I've never had to depend on him before," Mrs. Gunn later recounted. Chip ran off, explained what had happened and insisted that the neighbor come with him at once.

After hospital X rays revealed severe muscle strain, Mrs. Gunn was treated and returned home—with new respect for Chip's dependability.

Maybe you have never had to trust someone the way Mrs. Gunn did. But most people would like to be considered as trustworthy as little Chip. We can't know when such trust will be asked of us. But we can try each day to be worthy of confidence. And we can probably expect to reap as we have sown.

"I rejoice, because I have perfect confidence in you."   [2 CORINTHIANS 7:16]

⊷§ Holy Spirit, may we be persons who can be counted on.

Teenager Alice Knapp of Burke, New York, became a foster mother for her 4-H project. Her "baby" was a Labrador Retriever puppy she volunteered to raise until it was old enough to be trained as a guide dog.

In a cooperative program with Guiding Eyes for the Blind, 4-H members like Alice are given carefully selected puppies, bred for intelligence and good temperament, for their first year of life. Then the dogs are returned to the organization's training school in Yorktown Heights where they are taught to work together with a blind person until the two are a smoothly functioning unit.

The year in a foster home reduces costs while insuring that the puppies are well cared for.

Volunteerism takes many forms—raising a puppy, digging wells in a developing country, writing to men and women in prison. It also takes people and thought. You're a person. Have you given any thought to volunteering?

"Let us not grow weary in well-doing."
[GALATIANS 6:9]

⋅≫ Holy Spirit, show us ways to get involved.

INTERNATIONAL POLITICS is only the tip of the UN iceberg. World inequities and the human misery they spawn are the focus of over 75 percent of its work.

These are the kinds of facts behind General Assembly deliberations:

■ A poor Asian country cuts back development plans because export prices for its main commodity collapse.

■ An African country, forced to import food to prevent famine, has little left to spend for tools that could improve its crops next year.

■ Seventy percent of the world's people get only 30 percent of the world's income.

■ The net transfer of financial resources from rich to poor countries amounts to about one-thirtieth of the world's annual military expenditures.

■ Children in poor countries die of diseases that would not be fatal if the victims had enough to eat.

Where does our nation stand in the face of such need? What can you and I do? If voters insist, leaders will respond. Start insisting.

"Am I my brother's keeper?" [GENESIS 4:9]

◄§ Holy Spirit, help us to apply the Gospel message in the world as it is today.

FOR SOME PEOPLE, sudden retirement can be deadly, mentally and physically. Now the Swedish government has a plan to help workers "taper off gradually."

The plan, the most revolutionary in Europe, gives Swedes the years between 60 and 70 to change from full-time to part-time work, and then full retirement.

"It was unions, supported by doctors and psychologists, who said it would be better if people went into retirement slowly," said Kenneth Bratthall, legal advisor of the Ministry of Social Affairs.

Sweden hopes to prevent many of the sudden deaths that occur soon after retirement and eliminate the psychological problems of the increasingly large portion of the population over 65.

Tapering off sounds like a good idea. Sure, there are problems, but the institutions of our society are there to serve people and not vice-versa.

Is there anything you can do to help make one person's retirement a more pleasant experience?

"The sabbath was made for man, not man for the sabbath." [MARK 2:27]

᪥ Assist us to know priorities, Jesus, and to keep them straight.

CITY DWELLERS AND FARMERS are often at logger-heads. And part of the reason is that they seldom get together. The Agricultural Council of America is trying to change that.

As part of an effort by which 100 city families visit farms and vice versa, the Ira Drogins of Brooklyn visited the James Sloans in upstate New York.

The Drogins learned that farmers were getting only 19 cents of the 48 cents they paid for a quart of milk. But aside from economics, notions about city slickers and country bumpkins were quickly dispelled. The adults found common interests. The children got right into fun. All looked forward to the Sloans' getting to the city for their visit.

It's not enough to be "open-minded" about people who are different. To learn what we might have in common, we have to mix with them. Then we can discover how the diversity of human ways can be a God-given enrichment.

"As much as you can, aim to know your neighbors." [SIRACH 9:14]

❧ Lord, help us to get to know others just as they really are.

SUSAN SULLIVAN OF WINNETKA, Illinois, says, "If you can't ban the gun, ban the bullet."

Mrs. Sullivan and her Committee for Hand Gun Control had been thwarted by the argument that limiting a person's freedom to buy a weapon abridges his constitutional rights.

So they are taking a different tack. The Committee urges that bullets be controlled by the Federal Hazardous Substances Act. The group has asked a national products safety agency that sales be restricted to police, the military, licensed pistol clubs and guards.

"How can they talk about bicycles . . . being dangerous," asks Mrs. Sullivan, "and not bullets?" Advertising agency, J. Walter Thompson, will amplify her voice with a free public relations campaign declaring, "You Need a Bullet Like You Need a Hole in the Head."

It isn't enough to shake your head sadly at a problem. Speak up. You may get the support of others who react just as you do and are glad someone voiced their feelings.

"Do not refrain from speaking at the crucial time, and do not hide your wisdom."
[SIRACH 4:23]

Give us the courage, Lord, to move and not always leave constructive action to others.

A PROFESSOR AT THE University of Santa Clara decided to do something about the 10,000 persons who starve to death each week in our world.

Doctor Joseph Grassi sent a brief note to 100 faculty and staff members of the California university and invited them to join him in skipping one meal a week. His plan was to send $4 per person (a low estimate of the money saved by fasting) every month to buy food for the world's hungry.

Twenty people responded. Within six months, their number had doubled. And SKIP-A-MEAL (address: Santa Clara, CA 95053) was born. The non-profit group will send a monthly reminder to anyone pledging to skip a meal a week and donate the money to fight hunger.

One person involved more than 40 others in feeding the hungry. Given the size of the problem, it's a modest effort. Given the fact that it is so easy to do, it's an enormous possibility. How do you see it?

"I would give my bread to the hungry and my clothing to the naked." [TOBIT 1:17]

◦§ Jesus, when we feed the hungry, we are carrying on Your healing ministry.

EVER HEARD OF DIAL-A-JOKE? or Dial-a-Prayer? There's even Dial-a-Shoulder, for those who need a friendly voice to talk it over with.

Now it's possible to pick up your phone and dial Save-a-Marriage in the New York City area. A trained counselor will discuss marital problems, from deserting wives to how to cope with retired husbands who stay home all day.

Dr. Laura B. Singer, former president of the American Association of Marriage Counselors, founded the program. She strongly feels such hotlines can help save marriages.

Sometimes, what seems like a marital catastrophe today may seem a lot less traumatic tomorrow—if you can make it through the day. Call 212-799-0101. It just might help.

Come to think of it, maybe your shoulder is big enough for someone else to cry on. You'll never know unless you try it.

> "Bear one another's burdens and so fulfill the law of Christ." [GALATIANS 6:2]

    Give me a heart big enough to love, Father, and shoulders broad enough to help others with their burdens.

IN ONE HORRIFYING MINUTE, Frank Parkhill, a bus driver in Australia, combined heroism and skill to save 39 bus passengers before he died.

A passenger heard Mr. Parkhill say, "The brakes have gone." Then, in the 60 seconds before the crash, the bus driver swerved past a car, cut between a turning car and truck, turned a tight corner on nearly two wheels to miss a house, mounted the sidewalk and ricocheted off a fence, swerved between two lamp-posts, missed a car with four people in it, ripped up four trees, missed a narrow bridge, smashed a safety barrier and leaped a creek.

The bus finally plunged into a 20-foot ditch. The impact killed Mr. Parkhill. But all his passengers were saved. Said one survivor:

"He had done everything within his power to avoid harming anyone else."

Sometimes, we can wonder, "Does anyone really care?" People like Frank Parkhill remind us that some people do.

> "O man greatly beloved, fear not, peace be with you; be strong and of good courage."
> [DANIEL 10:19]

ᔊ Jesus, You were courageous in seeking God's will. Give us strength.

WE COULD BE IN THE DARK AGES, so far as two-thirds of the world's people are concerned. Advances in nutrition, health and education aren't reaching them.

Billions of dollars and three decades of effort haven't succeeded. But UNICEF and the World Health Organization are behind a worldwide plan to teach rural and shanty-town dwellers to do it for themselves.

Village workers, chosen by their own neighbors, are trained at central locations. They return to teach better infant care and how to grow nutritious foods from local sources.

Some learn basic medical techniques and find out when to refer serious cases to an area clinic. A study has shown that such simple measures could prevent 90 percent of infant deaths.

Help efforts to teach the poor. It is effective and it builds self-esteem. As in planting and nurturing a seed, such human solutions promote inner strength, growth and permanence.

> "Love one another with brotherly affection; outdo one another in showing honor."
>
> [ROMANS 12:10]

&⸗§ Father, may our efforts to help the needy nourish the whole person—body and spirit.

THERE'S A STORY AROUT A TRAVELER in Ireland, who met an elderly gentleman going in the same direction as he. They walked along enjoying the scenery together. Then a storm came up.

The two men took shelter, chatted awhile and eventually fell silent. Then the old man took out a small book and began to pray.

The traveler was struck by a certain air about the other man. And he said what he felt: "You must be very close to God."

The old man paused and smiled. Then he said, "Yes, He's very fond of me."

We are quick to offer reasons why people don't like us, or why their good opinion of us is mistaken. Sometimes we let real or imagined guilt lead us to believe that God is out to get us.

If we could really believe that He is "very fond" of us, we could relax a bit more, leave more in His hands and have time over to enjoy ourselves and be of real use to others.

"The steadfast love of the Lord never ceases." [LAMENTATIONS 3:22]

⊸ Holy Spirit, strengthen our belief in the Father's love.

Є VEN PROFESSIONALS TRAINED TO deal with death in health and religious fields find it hard to contemplate their own deaths.

When a survey asked 78 Canadian medical, nursing and divinity students to fill out their own death certificates, only 30 would do it. Those who did, saw themselves dying at an old age, quickly and not in the summertime. Most anticipated death by heart disease, at an average age of 70.3. Two said they would live to be 100.

None expected to die in June, July or August. Most thought they would die in winter.

"Some felt unable to fill them out at all," wrote the surveyor. "The results . . . show that a group of students in health professional training, even after considering death in the abstract, still project very unrealistic perceptions of their own death."

If we gave some thought to death, we might be more attentive to the way we live. The only time for compassion, work and faith is now.

> "In all you do, remember the end of your life, and then you will never sin."
>
> [SIRACH 7:36]

  Lead us to a healthy sense of our own mortality, Jesus, and help us face death as You did.

WHAT THEIR TOWN LOOKS LIKE means a lot to the inhabitants of Nivelles, Belgium, and they proved it at the polls.

When the town's medieval church was to have its tower restored, the choice of Romanesque or Gothic style arose. The issue was debated by art experts, but the final decision was made by the people.

Turning out in cold and rain, 61 percent of Nivelles' voters cast their ballots and opted for Romanesque. The tower will replace a Gothic spire lost in World War II, and will match the church's original style.

"When given the choice of what kind of environment they want to live in," said Nivelles' mayor, "people will respond."

Experts are important, but they can't replace the expressed needs of the people who have to live with what the experts plan.

It always pays to check at the grass roots. Given a chance, the people will make their views known.

> "We desire to hear from you what your views are." [ACTS 28:22]

✆ Give us a greater trust of people, Jesus, like You had in Your days on earth.

A 7-YEAR-OLD FILIPINO BOY has a whole restaurant staff in Lansing, Michigan, for a family.

When waitress Yeska Bruhl read about the foster child program for supporting youngsters in distant parts of the world, she wanted to help. But $12 a month seemed a bit steep for her budget.

She decided to interest the rest of the restaurant's staff. Both waitresses and kitchen crew responded gladly.

"Every month we send $12 to this boy—an amount we do not miss," recounts Ms. Bruhl. "To him it is a great deal. It means a little better food and, probably, shoes he might otherwise not have."

When people in other parts of the world are statistics, we don't feel inclined to help. But when "they" become one person in need, the way to constructive action is clearer.

Maybe there's a church group or other organization through which you can share your concern for a poor person or family. Why not try—today?

"Defend the cause of the poor of the people, give deliverance to the needy." [PSALM 72:4]

ᴥꜱ Make us aware of other peoples, Lord, in ways that are practical and personal.

HAVE YOU EVER THOUGHT OF what it must be like for handicapped persons on election day? How do they vote? Unfortunately, many never do.

Connecticut, among other states, is trying to make it easier for the disabled. They can use absentee ballots. Buildings used for voting purposes must have ramps for wheelchairs. And permanently disabled persons can get election officials to visit their homes to register them.

But many problems remain. Some polling booths are too small to admit wheelchairs. Names on the ballot are often too high to be seen. Even those services available may not be widely enough known.

As one man with cerebral palsy puts it: "You have to be a very determined person to vote."

Now that you know some of the difficulties handicapped persons must overcome to vote, is there anything you can do to help? And not only on Election Day, but every day.

> "Let each of you look not only to his own interests, but also to the interests of others."
> [PHILIPPIANS 2:4]

❧ Remind us, Lord, to think more about the problems of others, and to do more to relieve them.

THERE'S AT LEAST ONE LIBRARY in the country that seems to have no problem with stolen books.

It's the Blue River Library in a one-room cabin in a remote part of Oregon. The door is never locked. There are no library cards. No time limits. No fees. Sometimes, there's not even a librarian. A sign near a stack of blank cards asks readers to print their names, the date and the list of books they are taking.

A 65-year-old widow, Mrs. Frances O'Brien, started the library for people in four communities of the Upper McKenzie River country when she retired as school district clerk. That was eight years ago.

"Hundreds of books are borrowed each week . . ." says Mrs. O'Brien. "Yet I can count on my fingers the number of books that have never been returned."

There's no point in being naive about dishonesty. But we could trust more. Trust nourishes relationships. Trust gives others a chance to do better. Trust helps people to know they're worthwhile.

> "In quietness and in trust shall be your strength."   [ISAIAH 30:15]

     ⴺ§   May we take a chance, Lord, and help others to find the best that is in them.

T HE FLIP OF A COIN made Miles Nelson the new mayor of Clyde Hill, Washington. Both he and the incumbent, Liberino Tufarolo had gotten 576 votes.

According to state law, the toss-up became the determining factor.

"It's ridiculous to decide an elective office this way," fumed Mr. Tufarolo, as the two men waited for a county official to toss the coin.

Mr. Nelson, the challenger, shrugged, "It's the least offensive method to all parties concerned."

The coin fell. In a moment, it was all over. And chance had decided an election.

The supporters of the losing candidate who neglected to vote left the election to chance rather than choice.

The millions who culpably fail to vote are in effect letting our country's future depend on the toss of a coin. Isn't the effort to vote—and vote wisely—a small price to pay for the privilege of being a citizen?

"If you pursue justice, you will attain it."
[SIRACH 27:8]

᪣ Help me, Father, to do my part and make my decisions.

FOR TEENAGER HAL COHEN, shooting baskets is like eating peanuts—once he starts, he can't stop. In a dazzling shooting streak in Canton, New York, the high school student shot 598 consecutive baskets in an hour and a half.

"I just felt I couldn't miss," Cohen said. "I'd take three dribbles and shoot."

Beginning with a few onlookers in the gym at 5:30, Cohen had racked up 300 baskets by 6:00. People filed in to watch. The crowd swelled to 100. At the 599th throw, the ball rolled off the rim, and the streak was over.

Cheering fans later learned that Cohen's feat is probably the second highest free-throw score ever made. The world's record is 1700 baskets.

Hal Cohen started his streak by accident. He just wanted to shoot a few baskets. If you want to start a winning streak in some area of your life, better not be so casual. Prayer, thought and good advice are much more reliable than chance.

"Keep alert with all perseverance."
[EPHESIANS 6:18]

    ❧ Father, may we look for opportunities to be of service.

M OVE OVER, RUDOLF. Santas in Dallas ride motorcycles. Mostly shorthaul truckers and day laborers the bikers have a club called the African Bandits. And they decided to play Santa.

What started out as an outlaw club a few months before Christmas last year turned out quite differently. The 30 Bandits rustled up donations and distributed toys to children at Dallas Crossroads Community Center, the YMCA and several black churches.

Why the switch? "We all sat down and talked it over," said a spokesman named "Big John," "and decided to go the other way . . . We didn't want to ruin a good name."

And there'll be more Christmas toys this year. The African Bandits have a toy fund now.

The point at which a group or an individual takes a destructive or a constructive path can be fleeting. Then momentum builds quickly. Be prepared. Your influence at such a crucial moment may make the difference.

"Seek good, and not evil, that you may live." [AMOS 5:14]

 ◅ Father, may we be alert for opportunities to move things in a constructive direction.

Argument-solving is a tricky business for the supervisor. Executive Digest offers some suggestions which may apply to teachers and parents, too:

1. Don't just stand around and watch. Be aware of your own responsibility in the matter.

2. Don't threaten to throw them both out.

3. Don't let your emotions dominate you.

4. Don't let the problem get out of proportion. Give it only the time it deserves.

5. Listen to both sides of the story. Then review the facts with each person.

6. Check the stories. Then get the disputants together again and try to help.

7. Try to be fair.

8. Be the boss. You have the last word. If you must, use it.

There's no foolproof way to settle disputes. People who try to be just and impartial may not make any more friends than those who don't, but at least they'll know they were unpopular in a good cause.

> "Render true judgments, show kindness and mercy." [ZECHARIAH 7:8]

> ✎§ Move us to uphold the truth, Lord, even when it goes against the grain.

FIRE TOOK THE LIVES OF TWO GIRLS, aged 8 and 10, in Washington, D.C. At their funeral, they had a military honor guard.

When Sgt. Robert L. Griffin, stationed in the nation's capital, heard that Corita and Darlene Wheeler lost their lives in the blaze, he was deeply moved.

"All I could think of was, what if it had been my daughter?" he said. "So I called some of my NCO (non-commissioned officer) friends to see what we could do to help."

Sgt. Griffin found out that the Wheeler family was desperately poor. From shop owners at the Pentagon where he works, the soldier collected enough money to help the Wheelers pay the burial expenses. And he, along with 13 other service people, took part in the funeral.

Compassion can't restore a life. But at least it can soften the blow. In moments of need, we can be a comforting presence to persons who are bereaved.

"Do not fail those who weep, but mourn with those who mourn."   [SIRACH 7:34]

ᴇⴼ Inspire us to action, Lord, when we are able to relieve human suffering.

315 / NOVEMBER 11

JUVENILE COURT JUDGE Joseph Sorrentino of Los Angeles knows about standing before the bench.

A member of a street gang as a youngster, he was sent to a reformatory at 14, to jail at 16 and discharged from the Marine Corps for fighting at 18.

In an about-face, he went to night school, graduated from the University of California, Santa Barbara, and from Harvard Law School. The judge's experience of institutional conditions that harden youthful offenders inspires his conduct as a judge.

He recalls the exhilaration of strutting with fellow gang members, all dressed in shiny jackets. "It was like stepping into a comic book . . . It made us feel important." Then the murder of the gang leader shattered the illusion. ". . . We weren't comic book heroes."

Not all youths so successfully shake dependence on phony heroics. But they all look for heroes, real ones. A hero needn't be flashy, just someone to believe in, someone who stands for something, someone to look up to. Maybe you can be one.

> "Let us set an example . . . for their lives depend upon us." [JUDITH 8:24]

& Jesus, You were a hero who listened and suffered and cared. Fill us with Your Spirit.

A CHICAGO WOMAN'S DYING WISH to spend her last hours with her family in Baltimore fell upon deaf ears —until a small air transport company showed it had a heart.

No commercial airline in the Chicago area would permit Teresa Sadaukas aboard. This led a local television consumer affairs reporter to tell the story and to criticize the airline policy.

Lou Emery of the Rockford Motor Company, an operation with one Lear Jet, decided to act. He waived the $2,200 flight fee. Within a few hours of hearing the broadcast, Mr. Emery had the patient, who had only a few days to live, aboard his plane.

Ordinarily, Mr. Emery transports terminally ill patients in his specially equipped plane for a fee higher than that charged by commercial airlines.

One gracious act like this doesn't solve the problems faced by families of dying patients. But it could spur other airlines to make such trips less difficult. One person does make a difference.

"Do what is right and good."
[DEUTERONOMY 6:18]

᪵ Never let me underestimate the power of one person, Jesus, even if that person is me.

CHESTER IS THE B.M.O.C. at Washington's Bellevue Community College. But Chester isn't a football hero. He's a computer.

Chester is one of about fifty teaching computers around the country. His more formal name is Ubiquitous Dial Access Information Retrieval System. He relays lessons to students via telephone and television screen, with the help of his 24 tape decks and two video-tape decks.

Chester can tell corny jokes, teach German or shorthand, recite political speeches and sing rock 'n roll. He was originally meant for student use. But his unlisted telephone number spread by word of mouth, and now he's even getting fan mail.

A computer can be regarded as a friend or a cold, impersonal enemy. Just as we reflect God's image, our technology shows what we are like. Have you ever thought of the computer field as a place to change the world for the better?

"You yourselves are full of goodness, filled with all knowledge, and able to instruct one another."　　　　　　　[ROMANS 15:14]

꿢 Jesus, make us more alert to ways in which we can promote concern for people.

A CHURCH AND ITS PASTOR WELCOMED a teenaged thief "like a son" when he asked their forgiveness.

Calling the boy only "Joe," the Reverend H.A. Boone of Indianapolis, Indiana, said church members provided a job and clothing for the young intruder, who had entered the church twice, taken some canned goods, and bathed in the baptistry. He had left a note the second time apologizing because he was "desperate and hungry, with no place to sleep."

The pastor had then left this message:

"Dear Joe, We're very much concerned and want to help you. No one is mad . . . If you come again, please call us at the following number . . ." He did.

How easy do we find it to give—or ask for—a second chance? The truth probably is that we find it very hard. But it is one good test of whether our Christianity exists in practice, or only in theory.

"If you forgive men their trespasses, your heavenly Father also will forgive you."

[MATTHEW 6:14]

Enable us to dig deeper, Jesus, into our own motivations as we deal with other people.

IN CALIFORNIA, COURSES at one college range from geology to grasshoppers. It's College for Kids.

Bright, highly motivated youngsters from 4½ to 16 go to classes on Saturdays and late afternoons at the College of Marin near San Francisco. Parents, local school districts and the college share expenses. "In a world of diminishing natural resources," says coordinator Jessie Harsham, "we must . . . encourage the development of our best mental resources."

The most popular courses are computers, speed reading, electronics and marine biology. No grades. No I.Q. scores asked for. Children learn best, says one instructor, going at their own pace.

One 8-year-old boy had a passion for electronics, but couldn't read. He worked at his own pace, blossomed and soon rose to straight A's in his own school.

If teachers, parents and administrators pulled together more often, we'd probably have a lot more youngsters enjoying school.

Their learning is worth our effort.

> "What you have learned and received and heard and seen in me, do."
>
> [PHILIPPIANS 4:9]

~§ Remind us that education is our business, Lord.

JUDY SCOTT IS ONE OF HUNDREDS of blind people who have learned to ski.

"I always wanted to learn," said Judy, 28, "but I thought this was simply out of the question."

She learned to ski in a course run by Purgatory Ski Area near Durango, Colorado. There, she skied beside an instructor, who held a five-foot bamboo pole which she grasped for balance while learning. After a while, the pole was released and she followed verbal commands of when and which way to turn.

"It's fabulous," says Judy. "Imagine being in the open spaces, without noise except for the skis and snow. The whole system is based on faith in the instructor."

If faith in another human being can help a blind person ski, imagine what faith in God can achieve. Jesus said it could move mountains. What faith in God can accomplish is limited only by our willingness to risk trusting Him. Those who accept the challenge of letting God into their lives are in for an adventure that never ends.

"All things are possible to him who believes." [MARK 9:23]

Holy Spirit, make us men and women of faith.

W HEN HIS SCHOOL stopped sponsoring a holiday food drive for poor families, seventh-grader Elliot Weinstein took over the program himself and ran it until his high school graduation six years later.

In 1969, Elliot decided not to let the school's Holiday Dinner Basket drive lapse, so he set up money boxes and asked fellow students to bring food items, which he turned over to the Paramus, New Jersey, welfare director for needy families.

Often Elliot collected enough to supply full-course dinners for 12 families.

"When I see the end result, it really makes me feel good," he said before his graduation. "I hope someone will take up the project next year."

We can throw up our hands in despair at all that's wrong with the world. Or we can do what this youngster did—look around us and take on a constructive job that needs doing.

If you want to feel good—and help others—the choice is obvious.

> "They are to do good, to be rich in good deeds, liberal and generous."
>
> [1 TIMOTHY 6:18]

    Holy Spirit, show us where there is work that needs to be done.

Two teenaged boys in Chappaqua, New York, had some explaining to do about the red-spotted walls when their parents returned from a vacation.

Steven and Lawrence Bock were left to care for the house, themselves and Baron, their Weimaraner.

One night, as Lawrence tells it, "Baron came in and started running around the room . . . he smelled bad." Clearly, the dog had met a skunk.

The boys learned from a veterinarian that liberal applications of tomato juice would neutralize the odor. They got to work but hadn't counted on the now Red Baron vigorously shaking his wet pelt. The skunk caper ended in the tub, and the walls en route to the bathroom were liberally spattered.

No wild parties, just Baron and the skunk.

With parents gone, youngsters can get into complications. But most want to be trusted. Start early encouraging responsibility. It gives children a chance to learn how good it feels to seriously contribute to the family.

"No greater joy can I have than this, to hear that my children follow the truth."
[3 JOHN 1:4]

❧ Father, may I give children in my care a real chance to mature.

To one New York psychiatrist, cooking is "the greatest therapy on earth."

Dr. Louis Parrish, a general practitioner and psychiatrist, says, "I spend a long day listening and talking to patients, and when I get home at night the first thing I do is rush to the kitchen."

Dr. Parrish, author of a book on the change of life in men and women, prefers improvised dishes and makes many specialties from leftovers.

"I tend to avoid overwrought dishes, but I have a passion for making my own fritters," Dr. Parrish says. Then he adds thoughtfully, "Someday I'll do a book on the therapeutic value of cooking."

Some mental and emotional problems require extensive treatment. But many yield to a greater involvement with the world around us. Cook a fritter, plant a flower, make a phone call. Whatever else happens, at least you won't be sitting around getting on your own nerves.

"Arise and be doing! The Lord be with you."
[1 CHRONICLES 22:16]

ᐧᔐ Lord, help us to achieve peace of mind.

AN UGLY AND DANGEROUS irrigation ditch became a mini-park when the women of Torrington, Wyoming, took action.

The weed-filled, century-old waterway ran through a 13-block residential area. The sole water supply to outlying farms, the ditch was the site of drownings and litter.

Then, the women of Torrington's garden club drew up a plan to make the ditch into a park. They took their plan to city officials with the owner's agreement to donate the ditch to the town. A $99,000 park bond was passed, and federal funds were obtained.

Farmers still get their water, but through a concrete irrigation pipe so efficient that Torrington saves 1,200 gallons of water each minute of the day. And there is a park instead of an eyesore.

Can you name one eyesore in your neighborhood? Can you think of three other people who might help you try to get rid of it? That may be all it takes. But one person has to say "go."

"She has done what she could." [MARK 14:8]

  Never let us forget, Jesus, that there's always something we can do to make our world better.

A MAN FROM BELLINGHAM, Washington, tried some lute music on his guitar and wondered what it would sound like on the real thing.

Because he couldn't buy a lute, John Rollins decided to make his own. It was a painstaking process. To his surprise, he found others wanted lutes and has begun building them for sale. He has orders five months ahead.

"More than 30,000 pieces of music have been written for the lute," says Mr. Rollins, "Some of them have not been played for hundreds of years, simply because there has been no one to play them and nothing to play them on."

Persistence can have surprising results. When it is directed toward objects that may give pleasure or service to others, such determination can pay off handsomely.

We might spend a few minutes each day asking how we could "make beautiful music" for people.

> "If even lifeless instruments, such as the flute or the harp, do not give distinct notes, how will anyone know what is played?"
> [1 CORINTHIANS 14:7]

ⅇ§ Draw us to Yourself, Jesus, and lead us into fresh ways of reaching out with Your love.

JACK FORTUNE OF EASLEY, South Carolina, got so caught up in the Bicentennial spirit that he placed an ad in the London *Daily Mail* to thank the British people for their good will to America.

"Thank you people of England," it read, "for the tribute you paid us on our 200th birthday. To you we owe our basic system of laws, justice and freedom."

"The response was astounding," he said later. "It gives me goose bumps." Mr. Fortune has received letters from members of Parliament and postcards and pictures of the Queen. All the letters, he said, were favorable to the United States.

To thank the British people for their response, Mr. Fortune has taken a second ad in the *Daily Mail*.

People like to be thanked. And it's so easy to do. Gratitude needn't cost a cent—or even inconvenience us. It can take as little as two words, "Thank you." So small. And yet they convey a whole world of meaning. Why not use them today?

"Be thankful."   [COLOSSIANS 3:15]

~ Jesus, You were a grateful person. May we never be too busy or thoughtless to say thanks.

Teenagers and senior citizens work together in the Lenox Hill Neighborhood Association's Project SCOPE, an outreach program for the elderly in New York City.

SCOPE supplies attention, food and medicine to the elderly in their homes. Senior aides determine needed services and arrange for meals-on-wheels, Medicare and Medicaid applications and doctor's visits.

Teen project workers help clean house, pick up prescriptions, chat and read to their new companions, often making three or four visits a week.

"We are needed," says Edith Morton, a senior aide. "I never stop."

Massive government funds and an army of professionals probably couldn't do as well what this small group of citizens is doing for themselves. You can't buy —or hire—the human touch. And that's a quality any of us can add to our service of others. It's a way of loving our neighbor as ourselves.

"Owe no one anything, except to love one another." [ROMANS 13:8]

    Father, help us to bcome more loving.

WHEN JOHN AND JANE SHUTTLEWORTH risked their entire savings of $1,500 on a "back-to-nature" magazine, in 1970, they didn't know it but thousands were waiting.

The Shuttleworths' savings barely paid printing costs of the first 64-page issue of *The Mother Earth News*. Now a 132-page bimonthly, "Mother" is a $2-million enterprise, including a syndicated radio program and newspaper column, a mail-order catalogue and a sister publication, *Lifestyle*.

The basic message is "consume less and enjoy it more." Articles stress the do-it-yourself-use-it-up-wear-it-out theme. Says John Shuttleworth, "We're all going to have to start going forward in a slightly different direction than we have in the past."

Most of us probably consume more and enjoy it less. Trying the opposite makes good sense, puts us more in tune with the Gospel, is cheaper and healthier. In fact, doing with less has everything in its favor except for the inertia that holds us back.

> "Let not your hand be extended to receive, but withdrawn when it is time to repay."
>
> [SIRACH 4:31]

⋞ Jesus, You knew the things that were important in life. Teach them to us.

WHAT YOU DON'T KNOW ABOUT BLOOD donation may be keeping you from being a donor. Dr. Robert Richmond, director of Baltimore's Red Cross Blood Center, cites the most common questions and their answers:

■ How much blood do they take? A pint.

■ How much blood does a person have? Ten to 13 pints.

■ How soon does the body replace the lost pint? Plasma volume becomes normal immediately; red blood cells in about 10 days.

■ Does high or low blood pressure disqualify? Not at all. Blood donating is a harmless process.

■ How long does a blood donation take? With a brief physical, medical history, and a "snack break" afterwards, just about one hour.

■ Does it hurt? As much as a momentary pin-prick.

If more people donated blood, it would become much cheaper for those who need it. And it would eliminate the practice of selling it for profit.

Giving blood doesn't hurt. And it really helps!

"Give graciously to all the living."
[SIRACH 7:33]

⌁ Spur us to seriously consider donating our blood, Lord, because others need it.

AFTER 40 YEARS OF WORK, Canadian zoologist Fred Urquhart has proved that Monarch butterflies migrate across a continent each winter. He has tracked the insects to a 20-acre region 9,000 feet above sea level, in the mountains of Mexico.

For years, Dr. Urquhart and volunteers tagged thousands of Monarchs, asking finders of the butterflies to notify the Zoology University of Toronto. Tagged specimens showed migration routes which pointed to Mexico, then disappeared.

Ads in Mexican papers for butterfly spotters brought a report from Kenneth Brugger, who had spotted the elusive Monarchs in a mountain area. A butterfly with a tag was found—proof of the delicate creature's astonishing cross-continental flight.

Birds and butterflies—and all animals—unerringly follow the route the Creator has given them. We're different. We can choose to stray from the path. If you do, hurry back. A loving Father waits to receive you with open arms.

> "The highway of the upright turns aside from evil; he who guards his ways preserves his life." [PROVERBS 16:17]

⊷ Jesus, remind us of God's unceasing love for us.

IT ISN'T EASY TO FIND A USE for a 750-pound sugar cookie.

A thief in Grand Forks, North Dakota, discovered this when he stole a rental truck at three o'clock one morning. After he had made his getaway, the thief opened the truck and found the monster cookie. It measured three feet wide, four feet long and two feet high, with Merry Christmas inscribed on it in pink frosting.

The thief abandoned his loot later in the morning, and police returned it to the manager of a local restaurant who was entering it in a contest.

One way to keep people honest would be to have nothing worth stealing. But that's obviously impossible. Real honesty comes when each of us decides to heed the divine command—"Thou shalt not steal." In other words, an honest world starts with you and me.

> "All who act dishonestly are an abomination to the Lord your God."
>
> [DEUTERONOMY 25:16]

ê§ Holy Spirit, may we render to everyone his or her due.

CHRISTMAS WAS COMING. People were out of work. Pupils in an all-black parish decided their usual distribution of food baskets was not enough.

With 30 percent unemployment, Holy Angels Parish on Chicago's South Side was hurting. So 800 youngsters wrote personal letters to local businessmen asking them to help.

"There are many people out of work in my neighborhood," Tiannia Easter, 9, wrote to the Peoples Gas Company, "but I would like you to hire just one for me." Commenting on the innovative approach, a department manager for the company was one of many recipients who were moved. "Luckily," he said, "we had some positions coming open."

The Children's efforts netted jobs for some 80 people in a number of firms.

When people are in need, a job means a lot more than a handout. Do you know anyone who could use a job? Do you know of any job openings, even part-time? It's worth making the effort.

> "What does the Lord require of you but to do justice, and to love kindness."
>
> [MICAH 6:8]

&ℑ Keep reminding us, Jesus, that one of the best things we can give anyone is the chance for self-help.

FOR GEORGE AND JANET KEATON's new baby boy, the rest of life is bound to be an anti-climax. After his exciting birth, anything would seem dull.

Racing through traffic to take his wife to a Charleston, West Virginia, hospital, George Keaton swerved to avoid a stream of cars. Out of control, his auto veered into the Elk River. As it sank, Mr. Keaton managed to push his wife through the broken windshield, and then saved himself.

Less than two hours later, at Charleston Memorial Hospital, Janet Keaton gave birth to a 6-pound, 2-ounce son. The attendants said that both "mother and child are doing fine."

Most people don't enter the world amidst such chaos. But we all hit days when things seem to come unglued.

In such moments, the values and habit patterns we have formed in quieter times really pay rich dividends. We prepare for our "big" day, by living our "little" days as well as we can.

"Now may the Lord of peace Himself give you peace at all times in all ways."

[2 THESSALONIANS 3:16]

  Holy Spirit, help us to remain serene amid the day's many clamors.

SOMETHING WAS WRONG. A Georgia school teacher became aware that one of her pupils was just not with the rest of her class.

So a counselor for the Gwinnett County Schools was alerted. She learned that the little girl's mother was dying and under sedation. The child felt lost, not knowing how to communicate with her mother.

"I touched her arm," said the counselor, Mary Jo Hannaford, "and suggested that we not say anything aloud to each other, and see if she could tell me what I was saying to her."

"She told me that I was saying that I loved her . . ." The counselor explained that, in the same way, she could tell her mother how she felt. The child's performance in school improved noticeably.

Feelings need expression. Sometimes a glance, a smile, a touch can be more expressive than words. To help someone learn how to communicate warmth and understanding might change that person's life.

> "That their hearts may be encouraged as they are knit together in love."
>
> [COLOSSIANS 2:2]

&ε May I be alert, Holy Spirit, when I can be the means by which Your love reaches a child.

HOW MUCH IS YOUR HOME TOWN linked with towns and cities throughout the world? A group of professors and graduate students in Columbus, Ohio, decided to find out. The results surprised local citizens.

Columbus, with a population of about a half million, yielded these statistics:

- 1,190 businessmen traveled overseas.
- 29,000 air tickets were bought for flights from Columbus to foreign cities.
- Nearly 100,000 hours per month were spent on international activities.
- Students from India alone numbered 125.

The aim of the effort was to stress the interdependence of the community with the rest of the world and to lead citizens to take a greater interest in world affairs.

A world community is emerging. Our interest in global issues and promoting justice and harmony can contribute to peace.

> "Let us then pursue what makes for peace and for mutual upbuilding."
> [ROMANS 14:19]

&§ It is Your world, Father. Strengthen our resolve to make it our world too.

Buying toys for children is becoming more and more of a challenge.

Heavy plastic wrappers used to protect items turn out to be a barrier to inspection. Contents, safety and suitability are not always as described on the package.

The Federal Trade Commission suggests that, if possible, you buy only toys you can inspect. Also, reduce the safety hazard of an unsuitable toy by seriously considering the child's age. Consider buying the "real" instead of the "play version," especially for hobbies. Quality is usually better.

Unsafe toys should be reported to the U.S. Product Safety Commission, Washington, D.C. 20207. Deceptively packaged toys should be reported to the Federal Trade Commission, Washington, D.C. 20580.

Play is the work of children, someone once said. How important, then, is furnishing youngsters with the right tools. A good toy, carefully chosen, is a powerful way to tell a child, "I love you."

"I will rejoice in doing them good."
[JEREMIAH 32:41]

  Jesus, inspire creative people with high ideals to enter the toy industry.

Deidre Garton, 24, found a way to combine her two major interests—the care of children and the practice of law.

Mrs. Garton, a mother of two, enrolled in a seven-week course in career counseling at MORE for Women, Inc. in New York.

She was asked to list the 50 main accomplishments of her life—anything from having the best valentine in second grade to learning the guitar to mastering Chinese cooking.

From her list, she then selected the ten that meant the most to her. Interest in children and the law kept showing up. After her husband completes his graduate studies (and can care for the children), Deidre Garton plans to study law and work with a social agency where she can do family law.

For most women, it used to be either a family or a career. Today, both are increasingly possible. It is a good trend for women themselves, their families and the society that needs their services.

"There are varieties of service, but the same Lord."   [1 CORINTHIANS 12:5]

✑ Make us more positive in seeking to find remedies, Holy Spirit.

A CALIFORNIA MAN BECAME a millionaire in one Christmas season by marketing "pet rocks."

The phenomenon has caused some to be angry at being "put on." Others shake their heads wondering "what we're coming to." Gary Dahl, the man behind the rock, packages the egg-shaped beach stones in a little doggie carrying case with breathing holes—for $4.

A manual tells how to care for your rock. It can be taught, it says, many things. To Sit. To Stay. To Roll Over—best taught on the side of a hill, advises the guide. To Play Dead—rocks love to practice it on their own. There's more.

"People are so . . . tired of all their problems," says Mr. Dahl. "This takes them on a fantasy trip—you might say we've packaged a sense of humor."

Whether or not you like the idea of a "pet" rock, it does show what a little imagination can do with the ordinary things in life. Try to stay open to the humorous. Your attitude may brighten life for someone else as well.

"Our mouth was filled with laughter, and our tongue with shouts of joy." [PSALM 126:2]

৵৽ May we bring joy, Lord, into our own lives and the lives of those around us.

Here's THE WAY FOUR FAMILIES in Birmingham, Alabama, prepared their children for Christmas one year.

"We got together," writes one of the mothers, "and gave a party for all of our children at which they wrapped their own toys to give away. We read to them from our Bibles about what Jesus said about love and giving and we saw some beautiful responses on their faces . . .

"When all the things were wrapped, we took the children and the gifts to the home of a fatherless family, with 16 children.

"They understood that they were not taking these gifts to show that they were good boys and girls, but rather because Christ could show love through them. They were humble, and I don't think that they will ever forget the experience."

Children learn by doing. So do adults. What better way to celebrate Christmas—and grow more God-like ourselves—than to share with someone else?

> "This is My commandment, that you love one another as I have loved you."
>
> [JOHN 15:12]

   Help us, Lord, at Christmas, a time of enchantment, to teach children the magic of love.

VERYBODY HAS MOODS—those ups and downs when days seem either rosy or black. Dr. Lilian Winer, a psychiatric social worker, offers these tips on handling moods—both yours and those of others:

- Face and deal with your mood.
- Look at yourself in perspective.
- Be inner directed, with life principles.
- Recognize unexpected problems when they hit you. If you can't solve them at once, go on with what you have to do.
- Try to keep a balance between thinking and feeling. Are you overreacting to events?
- Remember, you don't always have to feel happy.

One of the most reassuring trends in psychology today is the increased emphasis on the fact that it's all right to be less than perfect.

God made us human—with flaws as well as good points. Accepting ourselves as we are is a big first step in becoming what He wants us to be.

> "It is my prayer that your love may abound more and more, with knowledge and all discernment." [PHILIPPIANS 1:9]

  Jesus, teach us to love ourselves—and each other—limitations and all.

THE LATE CARDINAL CUSHING of Boston prayed:
"Slow me down, Lord! . . . Steady my hurried pace
with a vision of the eternal reach of time.

"Give me, amid the confusion of the day, the calm-
ness of the everlasting hills.

"Break the tension of my nerves and muscles with
the soothing music of the singing streams that live in
my memory . . .

"Teach me the art of taking minute vacations—of
slowing down to look at a flower, to chat with a friend,
to pat a dog . . .

"Let me look upward into the branches of the tower-
ing oak and know that it grew great and strong because
it grew slowly and well . . .

"Slow me down, Lord, and inspire me to send my
roots deep into the soil of life's enduring values . . . that
I may grow . . . toward the stars of my destiny."

Busy or not, it's good to be still and listen. It is in
the silence of the heart that God speaks.

"Be silent before the Lord God!"
[ZEPHANIAH 1:7]

   ☞ Father, remind us, once in a while, to slow
     down.

IN ELSINORE, CALIFORNIA, junior high students know they can look to Mrs. Bertha Feeley for understanding.

Mrs. Feeley is the school's liaison worker with the Chicano (Mexican-American) community. Her job involves getting to know students and their families, and helping with their problems.

The bi-lingual mother of eight finds it easy to relate to students and their parents because she has lived in Elsinore 21 years.

Principal Fred Quigley, who hired Mrs. Feeley to help break down barriers between the school and community, credits to her a 33 percent drop in absenteeism.

It's amazing how much can be achieved by one person who cares. On second thought, it's more amazing that more of us don't make the effort. Somewhere, today, someone needs your love. Ask God. He'll point you in the right direction.

"Let us consider how to stir up one another to love and good works." [HEBREWS 10:24]

❧ Father of all, help us to love one another in action.

IN HER COLUMN, Ann Landers quoted "The Ten Commandments of How to Get Along with People":

1. Say less than you think. Cultivate a soothing voice—how you say it often means most.

2. Make promises sparingly; keep them faithfully.

3. Never lose an opportunity to say a kind word to or about somebody. Praise work well done.

4. Be interested in others. Let everyone you meet feel that you regard him or her as important.

5. Be cheerful.

6. Keep an open mind on all debatable questions. Discuss, but don't argue.

7. Let your virtues speak for themselves; refuse to discuss the shortcomings of others.

8. Respect the feelings of others. Wit and humor at the expense of a friend is never worth it.

9. Pay no attention to personal attacks on you.

10. Don't be concerned about your "just due."

It's all in Jesus' commandment, "Love God . . . Love your neighbor."

"Love one another, just as He has commanded." [1 JOHN 3:23]

Father, help us to treat each other like brothers and sisters.

Five miles a day is just an ordinary outing for 99-year-old Herman Smith-Johansen, named Dubonnet skier of the year in Canada.

Mr. Smith-Johansen lives in Quebec. But he learned cross-country skiing in his native Norway. Recently, he joined a ski trip involving daily 10-mile excursions. He dropped out after the first 10 miles, not from fatigue but because his daughter tore a ligament on the first day of the cross-country trip.

During World War II, when he was averaging 1,500 miles a year on skis, the hardy Norseman tried to volunteer for the Mountain Ski Corps. He was turned down because of his age—67.

Age, responsibilities to family and employer, physical capacity—those and other factors can limit our choices of what to do with our lives. But the biggest restriction is probably our own attitude. The choice—under God —is ours; to live or simply to exist.

"But it is the spirit in a man, the breath of the Almighty, that makes him understand." [JOB 32:8]

  Jesus, You lived life to the hilt. Guide us in Your footsteps.

TAKE A BASKET OF SURPLUS military parts and one junk auto body, and what do you have? Dick Bassett made them into an electric car that hums along at 40 m.p.h. for less than a penny a mile.

Mr. Bassett, an Albuquerque, New Mexico, engineer, spent $1,000 for 10 lead-acid storage batteries, electrical parts and a car body. Stripping the car of its motor and radiator, he put in the batteries and a generator.

"The idea of an electric car isn't anything new," he says, "but putting one together and driving it around town sure is. No power is consumed. An overnight charge is sufficient to restore even a completely dead battery."

Ours has been called the "throw away society" because of the rate at which we use and discard the earth's resources. Dick Bassett—and people like him —show that this need not be the case. A little thought will show ways in which we can conserve resources.

> "We can hardly guess at what is on earth, and what is at hand we find with labor."
> [WISDOM 9:16]

   Father, You made the earth. May we cherish it.

HELEN KELLER WAS BORN BLIND and deaf. Her words reflect the courage and wisdom with which she lived her full life. Among them:

"Security is mostly a superstition. It does not exist in nature, nor do the children of men as a whole experience it.

"Avoiding danger is no safer in the long run than outright exposure. Life is either a daring adventure, or nothing.

"Serious harm, I am afraid, has been wrought to our generation by fostering the idea that they would live secure in a permanent order of things . . .

"Before it is too late they must learn and teach others that only by brave acceptance of change and all-time crisis-ethics can they rise to the height of superlative responsibility."

It's not always easy to have the courage to face each day as it comes from God's hands. But it is possible. Maybe for you—as for Helen Keller—life can also become a daring adventure.

"Be strong and of good courage."

[JOSHUA 1:9]

⋦ᷤ Give us courage, Lord, to listen to Your voice within us rather than to the confusion around us.

ONE FAMILY'S THREATENED MORTGAGE foreclosure touched off a parish save-a-home program in a New York community.

When a series of financial reverses left a Lake Ronkonkoma parishioner destitute and facing eviction from his home at Christmas, Father John Carew of St. Joseph's Church did something about it. Remembering a similar program during Depression days, Father Carew announced plans for a Save-a-Home fund.

Churchgoers greeted his appeal with gifts totalling $5,000—enough to stall the foreclosure and even to help others. And, says Father Carew, they "tore the place down with their clapping. I nearly fell out of the pulpit. I didn't expect it."

Some people talk a lot about "community." All of us live in a community. But the word comes alive only when people come to the aid of their neighbors.

Is there need in your neighborhood that you can help fill? It only takes one person—maybe you—to begin. Today.

> "Insist . . . that those who have believed in God may be careful to apply themselves to good deeds." [TITUS 3:8]

> ❧ Remind us to do more to make homes of our houses, Lord, and communities of our neighborhoods.

CHRONIC ALCOHOLICS ARE SUFFERING from misguided kindness according to the head of a Syracuse, New York, rescue mission.

Clarence Jordan told New York state legislators that new shortened jail terms are getting many alcoholics back on the streets before they "dry out."

"Some of the men used to serve 30, 60, or 90 days," said Mr. Jordan. "Now the man is back on the street more often. We have actually seen men die."

One alternative Mr. Jordan cited was the Rescue Mission's special center to treat alcoholism, but such treatment centers are too scarce to be able to handle the widespread problem.

Enlightened attitudes toward alcoholism are becoming more common. It isn't enough, however, to stop treating drunkenness as a crime. We have to recognize it as a medical matter and provide appropriate facilities and treatment. This is lighting candles instead of cursing the darkness.

"Shine as lights in the world, holding fast the word of life." [PHILIPPIANS 2:15]

◆§ Father, bless those working in alcohol rehabilitation programs.

APARTMENT HUNTING IS DIFFICULT for anybody, but for the handicapped, it can be a nightmare.

"Finding a place to live is the biggest problem we have," says Danny Franklin, an Atlanta, Georgia, draftsman confined to a wheelchair. He says few apartments have low enough cabinets, sinks and stoves, or wide enough floor areas or doors.

"We aren't talking about building housing for the handicapped where they will all live together," Mr. Franklin said. "This has been tried, but the handicapped don't like it."

The problems of Danny Franklin and others like him are being studied by the President's Committee on the Employment of the Handicapped. But the awareness of special housing needs is late in coming, often not even mentioned in schools of architecture.

Wherever you can, remind others of the special requirements of handicapped persons. A little more thoughtfulness can enable many such persons to live and work as well as anybody.

> "Judge your neighbor's feelings by your own and in every matter be thoughtful."
> [SIRACH 31:15]

⋞ Increase our capacity for being considerate, Jesus, and spur us to do something about it.

POSTMARK WAS ONCE A FAMILIAR clue to a letter writer's identity, or at least good for a guess.

The sterile mark, "U.S. Postal Service . . ." on computerized mail cancelled all that. But Ray Geiger, owner of the *Farmers' Almanac,* has just won a campaign to bring back the postmark. "It's so important," says Mr. Geiger, "for people to see this little homey touch on an envelope."

He contacted 150 members of Congress, the top brass of the Postal Service and took off on a speaking and broadcasting tour of the country.

The Postal Service finally agreed to use the name of the appropriate mail-processing center.

What's more important, perhaps, than the return of the homey touch is the fact that someone can still take on the bureaucracy—and win.

The day nobody speaks up or takes a chance for what they believe in will be the last day for democracy. One person can make a difference!

"A word fitly spoken is like apples of gold in a setting of silver." [PROVERBS 25:11]

&ᶟ Never let us give up hope, Lord, in our power to effect change, or in Your support.

PSYCHOLOGIST PETE SMITH believes that your life is your own, and what happens in it is up to you.

Officially, Pete is Dr. Manuel Smith, a professor at U.C.L.A. His book "When I Say No, I Feel Guilty," expresses his confidence in personal responsibility.

He says, "I have faith in mankind, but not in other individual men to make decisions concerning my well-being. I am my own judge."

Self-assertiveness is unlike bullying or defensiveness, according to Dr. Smith. It is the ability to say, "I see things differently. This is important to me, and I am not going to fall apart."

After all, he says, "the first thing we do in life is protest, the moment we are born. That's our first independent act as a human being."

In many areas of our lives, we're not in charge. But where we can rightly assert ourselves, we'll probably be better off by doing so. Freedom is God's gift, but we are the ones expected to use it.

"Where the spirit of the Lord is, there is freedom." [2 CORINTHIANS 3:17]

⋖ᔕ Help us diminish our fears, Lord, and redirect wasted energies to constructive purposes.

EDGAR GOFF HEATS HIS OFFICE building with a well. The Bessemer City, North Carolina, businessman uses warm water drawn from the earth.

"The farther down you go, the warmer the water gets," Mr. Goff reasoned. "So, I thought, what's wrong with drilling a well and bringing up some of this heat from the earth."

After checking with engineers, miners and contractors, Mr. Goff sank a well 180 feet deep, drawing hot water to the surface by an electrical pump. It runs through a warmth-extracting device combining pressure and electricity to both heat and cool. The same hot water heats Mr. Goff's building in winter and cools it in summer, at a cost of about $1.15 a day.

Our current energy shortage is very real. But with inventiveness and flexibility like Mr. Goff's, we can find new sources of energy. Plenty of treasures are buried. Our job is to dig for them.

> "God called the dry land Earth, and the waters that were gathered together He called Seas. And God saw that it was good."
>
> [GENESIS 1:10]

☙ Father, keep us open to creative solutions to today's needs.

THE WHOLE WORLD IS A LABORATORY for the advanced biology class of a Syracuse, New York, high school.

Mrs. Barbara Spector of Nottingham High School, teaches the course without a text. Each student does original research, from electron microscopy to brain research on horseshoe crabs. The class examines such areas as law and behavior, religion and science, electronics and ethics. She uses visuals, tapes, reprints and lectures of famous guest speakers, and trips to hospitals, universities, a medical school and a local pharmaceutical firm.

"We need more courses like this," says Ernest Rookey, the principal. "It's a good comprehensive program that allows students to investigate many areas, preparing them to better choose their own futures."

The power of a teacher like Barbara Spector can't be estimated—or priced. You and I may not teach. But how about school budget votes? How about PTA? How about praying for teachers? If we choose to, we can make education our business.

> "Let your souls receive instruction; it is to be found close by."   [SIRACH 51:26]

      ⌀§   Holy Spirit, guide teachers as they reach young minds.

A FAMILY IN MISSION, KANSAS, hasn't exchanged Christmas gifts for 20 years.

It hasn't been easy, says Mrs. A. C. Cuppy, "while raising four boys in the midst of social pressures. We believe that since this is Christ's birthday, trading gifts with each other is inappropriate.

"All of our Christmas giving must be done to those who are in no way able to return the gift—'even the least of these.' We donate time and money to the . . . Christmas Store, where poor families can come and pick out what they wish to take home for their families . . ."

They say, says Mrs. Cuppy, that Santa Claus "represents the spirit of love and good will—why is Jesus Christ not adequate for that?"

If you find your traditional Christmas festivities a little empty, the original spirit lost, perhaps you, like many of us, have let the spirit of the market place take over.

"Jesus said . . . 'I am the way, and the truth, and the life.' " [JOHN 14:6]

✑ Jesus, may we honor Your birth by celebrating with a little more love.

THIS DEFINITION WON A PRIZE: "A friend is the one who comes in when the whole world has gone out."

Some psychologists comment on friendship:

Dr. George V. Coelho claims that friends are discovered rather than made. When you find a friend, you'll know it; he's been looking for you, too.

Dr. Sidney M. Jourard finds that in good friendships:

■ Each is concerned for the happiness and growth of the other.

■ Each can communicate honestly his thoughts, feelings, wants, memories and beliefs.

Robert S. Albert and Thomas R. Brigante report that "friends help us place on solid ground our thoughts, feelings, opinions and attitudes . . . Their support becomes part of the order and security we live by."

Friendship is precious. A friend is kind, not jealous, arrogant, selfish or resentful. A friend is ready to excuse, to trust, to hope and to endure. A friend loves. Be a friend.

"There is nothing so precious as a faithful friend."   [SIRACH 6:15]

৯৫ Help me, Lord, to be a friend.

A JUDGE WHO underwent open heart surgery paid for the same operation for a baby whose father had smuggled marijuana to pay for the infant's surgery.

Jackie Santiago, an 18-month-old toddler from Guadalajara, Mexico, will have her travel expenses and medical costs paid by Superior Court Judge Jack Marks. Judge Marks made the offer after Jackie's mother was deported and her father jailed for smuggling 1,200 pounds of marijuana.

Mr. Santiago, a U.S. citizen, pleaded guilty. He said he was trying to raise $10,000 for his child's surgery. Judge Marks made his offer on the fifth anniversary of his own heart operation.

"We're human beings first and judges second," he said. "When I learned that the child might only live for another year or so, I called for the surgeon."

Justice without mercy can be too harsh. Before we judge people's actions, it's a good idea to find out why they do what they do. Sometimes it can be an eye-opener.

> "May the Lord grant you wisdom in your heart to judge his people in righteousness."
> [SIRACH 45:26]

❧ Father, remind us to be slow to condemn and quick to understand.

Sᴀᴍ Wᴀᴛsᴏɴ ᴏꜰ Aᴛʟᴀɴᴛᴀ thinks "Christmas is such a lonely time." Several years ago he decided to do something about it.

With $30 in the bank and contributions from the public, the antique store manager fed 4,500 needy people in the hall of St. Mark's United Methodist Church.

By last year, he was calling it a 24-hour Marathon Christmas Party. Starting at noon on Christmas Eve, an estimated 6,000 people dined in the church hall. Turkeys, hams, chili, cakes and pies were donated by local individuals and merchants.

"I have a responsibility for these people," says Sam Watson.

Christmas is a time for remembering how much God cares for all peoples of the world.

It is a time for each of us to ask ourselves whom do we see as our responsibility?

Nothing says "thanks" to the divine generosity like a serious attempt to imitate it.

"If God so loved us, we also ought to love one another." [1 ᴊᴏʜɴ 4:11]

✌ Holy Spirit, help us to pass on the love You give us.

WHAT WOULD CHRISTMAS BE LIKE without Santa Claus? An American family manages just fine without him in the place where Jesus was born.

In Bethlehem in the Holy Land, Rev. Howard Carlson of Tacoma, Washington, administers a hospital financed by the Presbyterian Church. "Christmas seems closer to the essence here," says Rev. Carlson, "than in the West where it is very commercialized."

The family will cut its own Christmas tree from the Judean hillside mentioned in the Christmas story. Their turkey will come from an Israeli kibbutz.

Rev. Carlson and his family feel a deep sense of history and religion in the rocky, barren landscape. They will pray on Christmas at one of two sites said to be the original shepherds' fields—in a cave where Greek Orthodox priests built a simple shrine.

We can't all go physically to Bethlehem to find the true meaning of Christmas. But we can travel in our thoughts and in our prayers. If we do, we will find there "the Child and His mother."

"To you is born this day in the City of David a Savior, who is Christ the Lord."
[LUKE 2:11]

    Jesus, may our Christmas remain a joyous celebration of Your birth.

WHAT IS ONE OF THE MOST VITAL needs of aged persons? To keep communicating, according to Sister Mary Agelia of Westport, Connecticut. That's why she formed "conversation clubs" at several nursing homes.

Sister Agelia, 65, began with older nuns in her own convent. Now she has branched out.

A typical early session centers on the sense of smell. "What smells do you remember from your own kitchen?" she would ask women in their 80s and 90s.

"It's hard work," she admitted. "I have to pull and pull." She added that most nursing home staffs don't have time to give individual attention.

"These old people watch TV all day," she said. "I have one 98-year-old lady who hasn't really talked in years, but I'm getting her started."

You don't need a federal appropriation to talk with one person in a nursing home. And yet a small thing like that can brighten lives. Couldn't we try? It costs so little and does so much.

"Kindness is like a garden of blessings."
[SIRACH 40:17]

    In all we do, Jesus, help us keep the personal approach in view, as You did.

Many years ago in New Zealand, a Maori Indian known as "Warrior Brown" because of her violent temper when drunk, decided to join the Salvation Army.

One day, as she was addressing a group of other Maoris, one of them threw a potato and struck her in the head. A Salvation Army officer winced. Would Warrior retaliate? She picked up the potato, put it in her pocket and went on speaking.

Months passed. One day, Warrior Brown returned to the same Maori village bearing a small basket of potatoes. She stopped by the hut of the person who had struck her. She had cut up the potato, planted it, harvested the crop from it and was now presenting it to the thrower as a gift from the Lord.

Christians believe that the Son of God became human 2,000 years ago to heal our separation from God and among ourselves, and to show us how to love. He also challenged us to show each other.

> "By this all men will know that you are My disciples, if you have love for one another."
> [JOHN 13:35]

  Jesus, may we give each other the only real Christmas gift—love.

A FAMILY REUNION—with a difference—was held in Oakland, California. The 60 relatives who met had in common a genetic disease that killed many of its members before the age of 40.

Called the "Joseph illness," the malady was inherited from a single ancestor, Antone Joseph, a Portuguese sailor who jumped ship in San Francisco in 1845 to begin life in America.

Over a weekend, two doctors provided diagnosis and counseling for Antone Joseph's descendants.

In the past, said one of the attendees, "there was a lot of blame, guilt and secrecy. Our relatives just wouldn't discuss it."

"I have no fear if I can accept myself as I am," said another.

"All this has changed my life," said a third. "Everyone wants to get rich and famous. But when you don't have a lot of time, those things are not so important anymore."

What's important in your life?

"I am with you always." [MATTHEW 28:20]

ᴇᴈ Deepen and broaden our sense of values, Lord. We have only one life to live.

Miss P. L. Travers, author of the Mary Poppins books, is quite at home in Fairyland.

Does she see herself as a dreamer? "Fairy tales put me in touch with my inmost self," she says. "How could living with my inmost self be a dream? It is the greatest reality."

Miss Travers endorses the belief of a mother who wrote to her, "Everything you understand intuitively in childhood is ground out of you in the so-called 'adult world' . . . So with my 9-year-old daughter, I now return to Mary Poppins."

In her book *About the Sleeping Beauty*, the author suggests that what lies asleep in ourselves, screened by the externals of living, can give our lives fuller meaning—and delight.

The child in us, simple, honest and readily touched by wonder and delight, can be awakened. We'll be better persons if it is. Of children, Jesus pointed out, "such is the Kingdom of Heaven."

"Beloved, we are God's children."

[1 JOHN 3:2]

ھ May we remember, Father, that we are Your children.

James Chapman of Wisbech, England, lived a full life. He died a happy man at 103, according to his housekeeper.

Mr. Chapman kept up a vigorous pace to the end. At age 100, he decided to put some excitement into his life.

In his last years, he rode gliders, helicopters, balloons, racing planes and racing cars.

His last ride was in a submarine.

Traveling up in the air or under the sea may not be your idea of bliss. But whatever your age, are there some things you would like to do, things that you aren't doing only because of self-imposed restrictions?

It's worth the effort to list the activities you'd like to engage in before you die. If we have something to look forward to, chances are we'll be more interesting and pleasant people for others to be around. To serve God and be a good person, it isn't necessary to be dull.

"Make a joyful noise to the Lord . . . serve the Lord with gladness." [PSALM 100:1,2]

   Widen my horizons, Father, and give me a glimpse of the enormous world in which I live.

ARE YOU LIVING IN THE PRESENT? You might answer, "How else?" But novelist Margaret Strom Jameson says that most of us don't live in the "now."

"I believe that only one person in a thousand knows the trick of really living in the present; most of us spend 58 minutes an hour living in the past with regret for lost joys, or shame for things badly done (both utterly useless and weakening) or in a future which we either long for or dread.

"The only way to live is to accept each minute as an unrepeatable miracle, which is exactly what it is—a miracle and unrepeatable."

Learning to live life as it comes—minute by minute —is one of those goals that are so easy to talk about and so hard to achieve.

One place to start is to pick a period each day— however brief—when you will sit quietly, free from distractions. Give it a try. You just might find yourself, and God.

"Take heed, watch and pray, for you do not know when the time will come."

[MARK 13:33]

ᴥ§ Father, may we heed Jesus' advice "not to be anxious."